light and Rejoicing

A Christian's Understanding
of Jewish Worship

by

W.W. Simpson

Christian Journals Ltd. Belfast

First English edition by 1976 by Christian Journals
Limited, 2 Bristow Park, Belfast BT9 6TH

Copyright © Christian Journals Limited 1976

ISBN 0 904302 16 4

Cover photograph: Memorial to the victims of Nazi
persecution by Naomi Blake

Contents

For my grandchildren
in the hope that
it may one day help them
to understand why
their grandfather
was so involved with
Jews.

Foreword

In the topsy-turvy way in which things so often seem to happen in this life, having just completed the Postscript which appears on page 132 I turn at once to write this hopefully brief Foreword.

I want simply to say that this book is intended as a kind of thank offering for the enrichment that has come into my life as a Christian through my contacts, extending now over many years, with a host of Jewish friends and with their ways of life and worship.

While I am very conscious of its limitations, I have done my best to ensure that it is free from technical errors and inaccuracies. My hope is that it may encourage some of my fellow Christians to explore further a territory in which I myself have found such great reward. And should it come into the hands of any Jewish readers I hope that it may be of some encouragement to them to realise how much what is so essentially their own may benefit their neighbours also.

My indebtedness, not merely to other writers, but to so many of my friends, is beyond measure. I can only hope that those to whom I owe so much will know best how to read between the lines. There are two, however, to whom my special thanks are due. The first is Ruth Weyl to whose cheerful typing and re-typing of the whole has been added, in the discussion of its parts, the insight and understanding of one who knows from within the way of life it seeks to describe.

The second is one whose friendship I count it a high privilege to enjoy: Dr Immanuel Jakobovits, Chief Rabbi of the United Hebrew Congregations of the British Commonwealth, who has paid me the great compliment of reading the typescript and has been good enough to send me a letter which he has very kindly said I may print as a conclusion to this Fore-word. This I gladly and most gratefully do.

Dear Mr Simpson,

Your work over many years in the promotion of understanding between Christians and Jews has earned you the respect and esteem of a wide circle of friends among whom I number myself. Since assuming my office in 1967, we have worked together constructively, in harmony and understanding, mainly within the framework of the Council of Christians and Jews which you devotedly served as General Secretary for thirty-two years.

You will, of course, not expect me to endorse everything that you have written in your book about Jewish worship, for you have written as a Christian, writing for Christians. As you make clear in your book, you have introduced inter-pretations which are characteristically your own into a presentation of the facts which are not in dispute.

I welcome this opportunity of commending your book as an example of the way in which, as you have emphasised, understanding an appreciation of another's faith may deepen and enrich one's own faith. In this respect, your book seems to me in full accord with those recommendations of the successive Assemblies of the World Council of Churches and the Vatican Council (referred to in your concluding chapters), urging a greater understanding of the Jewish faith.

With all good wishes,
Yours sincerely,

Immanuel Jakobovits
(Chief Rabbi)

Beginnings

For me it all began quite a while ago. I was a student at the time, reading theology, which included the Old Testament and a little Hebrew, the New Testament and rather more Greek, and some Church history. It was all very interesting but at the time seemed to have very little bearing on my first encounter with a Jew.

He was at another college reading classics. We met in the rooms of a mutual friend whose first anxiety seemed to be that I might at once set about trying to persuade his Jewish friend that he ought to become a Christian. Once that fear was allayed he introduced me to Eric who was not only Jewish but orthodox as well. We got on very well together and it was not long before I was invited to a Friday (Sabbath) evening Service, and afterwards to a meeting of the Jewish Students Society, following the Sabbath evening meal.

The meeting was addressed by the visiting preacher, a distinguished rabbinic scholar who later became the first Chief Rabbi of the State of Israel. His subject was: 'Science and the Talmud', and since I knew little enough of the first, nothing of the second and had never previously thought of visiting a synagogue I quickly found a whole new world opening up before me, and the whole course of my life changed.

I had, of course, always believed that it is important to understand other people's points of view, to know something of their background and their way of life. That was the least they had the right to expect of me. This, had the question ever arisen, I should have recognised as applying equally to Jews as to anyone else. At that time (and I might as well admit that this was away back in 1928) it just hadn't.

At that time I knew nothing of antisemitism. Nor had it occurred to me how much a better understanding of Judaism and the history of the Jewish people might contribute to my own understanding of Christianity. So it happened that what at first looked like just another chance encounter between students became the starting point of a new, exciting and deeply enriching adventure.

It has had its dark side, of course. It would, I believe, be quite impossible to study the history of antisemitism as I have since found myself compelled to do, or to become as closely involved with some of its victims as I have been, without experiencing, as a Christian, a deep sense of shame and humiliation. For the tragic process which found its climax in the Nazi holocaust owes all too much of its origin and impetus to a certain Christian rejection of Judaism and the Jews.

But that is only one side of the story. For nowhere, I suppose, in the whole spectrum of human history has the silver lining shone more convincingly through the dark cloud than in the faith and courage of the

Jewish people. That has been especially the case in the Jewish home and the synagogue. Which is what this book is really about.

Certainly it explains the seeming paradox of the cover where the title 'Light and Rejoicing' is superimposed on a photograph reminiscent of the Holocaust, as indeed, it was intended to be. For the sculpture which is to be seen in the entrance hall of the headquarters of the Council of Christians and Jews in London, is the work of Naomi Blake who, as a girl, was in the Nazi concentration camp of Auschwitz. It was created as she herself put it, as a memorial to the victims of the Nazi Holocaust in Europe including six million of her fellow Jews. It is dedicated to the promotion of understanding and goodwill between people of different faiths and racial backgrounds.

Against this background the title echoes the spirit which inspires every aspect of Jewish life from its happiest to its saddest moments. For everything there is a blessing and in the presence of death itself the words which come instinctively to the mind and lips of every Jew are those of the so-called mourners' *kaddish*: 'Magnified and sanctified be his great Name in the world which he hath created according to his will'. Such faith stems from the earlier affirmation in the opening verses of the Bible itself: 'and God said, "Let there be light", and there was light'. And in that light, in which poets and prophets saw the eternal symbol of the divine presence, 'there is fulness of joy for evermore'.

The purpose of this book, then, is to explore something of the meaning of Jewish life and history for the average Jew, particularly through the medium of his

13

religious observances, both in his home and his synagogue. At the same time we shall be exposing ourselves to the possibility of discovering much that may prove helpful to the Christian in the understanding and practice of his own faith.

There is, of course, an initial difficulty. It is as meaningless to talk about 'the average Jew' as it is about the 'average Christian'. There are rich Jews and poor Jews, there are British Jews, American Jews and Jews of almost every nationality, including above all today, Israeli Jews. There are religious Jews of varying kinds, ranging from extreme forms of right-wing orthodoxy to progressive, left-wing, reform or liberal Jews. There are many Jews who profess to be non-religious, though relatively few who would go so far as to say that they were anti-religious. By non-religious they mostly mean non-observant in that they no longer go regularly to synagogue nor maintain the traditional religious observances in their home. This does not necessarily mean that they are irreligious. Many who no longer participate in the services whether of the home or the synagogue are deeply concerned about issues which can only be described as fundamentally religious. Much the same, of course, is true in the Christian community. This is one reason why mutual understanding between Christians and Jews is so important for both.

Here, then, I propose to interpret 'average' as applying to those who belong to the main stream of orthodox Jewish life, still participate in the life and worship of the synagogue and its related communal activities, and who still maintain at least the major religious observances which over so many centuries have so greatly enriched the life of the Jewish home and family.

14

And lest I be accused of omitting the 'warts' from what, at best, can be little more than a sketch, let me plead guilty at once. Christians have for far too long paid attention only to the supposedly negative and exclusive side of Judaism and Jewish life. They have ignored almost completely those creative and universal aspects which they assume all too easily to have been taken over by Christianity.

We shall not get very far, however, without realising that underlying all the questions relating to different types of Jews is the fundamental problem of the identity of Jews themselves. It is a problem as bewildering and embarrassing to many Jews as it is to their neighbours. The sophisticated and the cynical may think it:

> odd of God
> to choose
> the Jews,

while even the response:

> Oh no, it's not
> He knows what's what,

serves only to raise a host of further questions. So in the search for any kind of satisfying answer we are driven back to the beginning, if not of time, at least of the particular history of the Jewish people who, if the truth be told, have always been something of a problem to themselves no less than to their neighbours. It has to do with this idea of being chosen, of having a sense of vocation. People who feel 'called' to anything, whether as individuals or, as in this case, a community, can hardly help being a problem. There is something about their attitude to life, about their way of life even, that marks them out as different, and to be different can be dangerous. The way of the non-conformist has always been hard, and the 'dislike of the like for the unlike' remains a frequent cause of discrimination and persecution.

In this Jews are no exception. From their earliest days they were taught to think of themselves as a people specially favoured by God. Had he not delivered them from the Egyptians? And did not Moses teach them that they were to become 'a kingdom of priests and a holy nation' (Exodus 19:6)? Whatever they understood by this, at least it seemed to imply both a special function and a particular relation to their God.

Not that they were very clear about it themselves. Some, indeed the majority of them, quite understandably interpreted the idea of having been chosen in terms of privilege. Others, among them the greatest of their prophets, realised that there could be no privilege without responsibility. If they had been called it was not for their own sakes only. The priestly function of their kingdom, and the holiness of their nationhood was to be, as one of them put it: 'a light to lighten the Gentiles' (Isaiah 42:6).

There was nothing vague or abstract about this. According to their tradition, whether they thought of their vocation as being for their own sakes or for the sake of the wider family of mankind, it was primarily a call to live their life, as individuals and as a people, in accordance with what they believed to be a divinely revealed pattern: the *Torah*, given by God to Moses on Mount Sinai. *Torah* is a Hebrew word. Basically it means 'teaching' or 'instruction'. Unfortunately it was translated into English as 'law', and although

16

many of the precepts which comprised the 'teaching' invariably came to have the force of law, the word *Torah* itself always meant, and still means, something much more alive and creative. 'The commandment that I lay on you this day', said Moses, 'is not too difficult for you, it is not too remote. It is not in heaven, that you should say, "Who will go up to heaven for us to fetch it and tell it to us, so that we can keep it?" Nor is it beyond the sea, that you should say, "Who will cross the sea for us to fetch it and tell it to us, so that we can keep it?" It is a thing very near to you, upon your lips and in your heart ready to be kept.' (Deuteronomy 30:11-14).

In this sense the idea of *Torah* has remained gloriously comprehensive. It embraces both the broadest principles definable in the simplest terms (as for example that a man's whole duty consists in not doing to his neighbour what he would not wish his neighbour to do to him... a negative form of the 'golden rule' which has at least the merit of starting from where most of us are!) and the most minute instructions as to how a man should say his prayers, prepare his food or conduct his business. And all this, Jews believe, has been laid down by God, not just thought up by man.

To this way of life their neighbours, whether friendly or hostile, could not remain indifferent. And their neighbours were many and varied. For the Jews lived at the cross-roads of the ancient world. All the main highways from west to east and from north to south passed through their territory. There was no other way. They were, therefore, constantly subject to foreign invasion. They were also under constant pressure to move out. Whether involuntarily as captives or of their own free will Jews were destined to become citizens of the world. And wherever they went their way of life marked them out as a people apart.

Reactions varied. Some of their conquerors in particular deeply resented their refusal to conform; take the stories of Daniel and Esther for example. Some of their neighbours were attracted by a manifestly high moral standard of life and the concept of a God who clearly belonged to a very different order from any pantheon of pagan deities. It was indeed to the influence of the Jews as they spread throughout the Graeco-Roman world, many of them actively engaged in proselytising, that the early Christian missionaries owed much of their success. This is another of the strange paradoxes of history. Cornelius, the Roman centurion who played so important a part in the broadening vision of the early Church, was already a 'religious man, and he and his whole family joined in the worship of God. He gave generously to help the Jewish people, and was regular in his prayers to God' before he came into contact with Peter and the other apostles (Acts 10:2).

But there is another tragic side to the story. It is a commonplace of human experience that quarrels within a family go deeper, are more intractable, and produce more disastrous consequences than quarrels of any other kind. Certainly it proved so in this particular case, for the New Testament, in this one respect at least, is very much the story of a family quarrel. Jesus himself was a Jew in the fullest sense of the term. He was a 'son of the *Torah*' which, as he himself said, he had come 'not to destroy but to fulfil'. The New Testament which tells the story of his mission and its consequences from one point of view, however, is heavily loaded against 'the Jews'. But of this more later.

For the moment our concern is simply to meet the Jew in his home and in his synagogue, to see something of his traditional symbols and observances, and to get something of the feel and the flavour of the great festivals in his religious year. And all this we must attempt with the help of our imagination.

Trees of Life

'Poems' declared a ballad writer of a generation ago with perhaps undue modesty 'are made by fools like me'. He was on surer ground but in no way original when he added: 'but only God can make a tree'.

The fact is that trees have always been associated with the divine. 'The image of the Cosmic Tree or Tree of Life belongs to a coherent body of myths, rites, images and symbols which together make up what the historian of religion Mircea Eliade has called the "symbolism of the centre".' So writes Roger Cook in a fascinating and profusely illustrated study of the place of the tree in the great religious traditions of mankind. (*The Tree of Life*, Roger Cook, Thames and Hudson, p.9.)

The Bible of the Judeo-Christian tradition is a splendid example. It begins with a story of a garden in the middle of which stood a tree whose fruit, forbidden to man, had the power to make him 'like God, knowing both good and evil'. It ends with a dream of a heavenly city through which flows a river on either side of which stands 'a tree of life which yields twelve crops of fruit, one for each month of the year, and the leaves of the tree serve for the healing of the nations'. And between the two, for those with eyes to see and imaginations to illumine, trees play an important role in the whole process of revelation.

Very early in their history the Hebrews found themselves living among people who worshipped their gods 'on mountain tops and hills and under every spreading tree' (Deuteronomy 12:2). For the Hebrews, however, there could be no plurality either of gods or shrines. Out of the heart of a burning bush came a message to Moses about the uniqueness of their God. Their worship, moreover, was to be concentrated in a single sanctuary: the Tabernacle, the moving symbol of the divine presence as they journeyed through the wilderness, and, when they settled in the Promised Land, the Temple in Jerusalem.

Both in the Tabernacle and the Temple the symbolism of the tree played an important part. It is represented by a lampstand and made in the image of a tree originally with three branches on either side of a central stem, and later with eight branches. Known in Hebrew as a *menorah* and in Latin as candelabra (where *candela* stands for 'light' and *arbor* for 'tree') it is indeed a 'tree of light' and of life: for the two concepts are clearly and deeply related. For centuries it has been the Jewish symbol *par excellence*, and although today, the six-pointed 'star of David' has been incorporated in the Israeli flag and is widely worn as an article of personal jewellery, the *menorah* remains as the central feature of the coat of arms of the State of Israel and is to be found in every Jewish home and synagogue.

Not surprisingly this same symbol has found a prominent place in Christian imagery from the earliest days of the Church. Of this there is no more splendid example than the massive twin candelabra which stand on either side of the centre aisle of Westminster Abbey, just inside the great west door. The work of a distinguished Jewish sculptor, Benno Elkan, a refugee from Nazi persecution, they represent on the one side scenes from the Hebrew Bible and on the other from the New Testament.

The *menorah*, however, is only one among many symbols we are likely to meet in the Jewish home or synagogue, and symbols, unless properly understood, can be both misleading and dangerous. The word symbol itself is Greek in origin. It was used for a mark or a token, a ticket, a watchword, an outward sign or a covenant. Its root meaning has to do with throwing things together, for purposes of comparison or suggestion. Like many another word, however, it has come to have a deeper meaning. Thus, for example, in his Bampton Lectures for 1968 (*Traditional Symbols in the Contemporary World*) Canon F.W. Dillistone draws an important distinction between symbols and signs (p.162 f.):

> The most striking division in the scientific world today is between those who become obsessed with the conception of ordered system, controlled system, mechanically functioning system, man the slave within the system—all this being expressed through an exact, unequivocal one-track system of conventional *signs*—and those who are prepared to work with an open system, a system in which indeterminacy, randomness, disorder, uncertainty are not only tolerated but are seen to have an essential part to play for the continuance of life and creativity—all this being expressed through a system of *symbols* which allow scope for personal imagination and guess-work in the human consciousness as well as for probabilities and indeterminate processes within the empirical world.

This distinction between sign and symbol is of great importance. Preoccupation with either to the exclusion of the other is a sure road to disaster, for the two 'systems' are essentially complementary. For the scientist, obsessed as he may so easily become, with the precise definition of what is precisely known, to ignore the imaginative and symbolic approach to questions to which neither his microscope nor his telescope, nor any scientific experiment yet devised, seem capable of providing an answer is just as dangerous as it is for the man who is prepared to let his imagination run riot with symbolism to ignore such 'facts of life' as the scientist has succeeded in laying bare.

There is another danger also to which those who find delight and inspiration in symbols are constantly exposed. It is that the symbol itself may all too easily become a substitute for the truth it exists to express however inadequately: the danger that the mere performance of a religious rite or ritual act may become an end in itself. This danger was from the beginning endemic in Judaism with its highly developed system of symbols and ritual observances. The prophets and the Rabbis were constantly warning people against it. Jesus was equally emphatic in his condemnation of what he described as 'hypocrisy'. By which of course he meant not conscious dissembling, but that deep rooted subconsciously motivated pretence which is so much a part of all our living.

It is a danger equally endemic in Christianity. It is very important that the Christian, as he seeks to enter into the spirit and intention of Jewish worship, should pay due regard to the beam in his own eye lest he become too hyper-sensitive about the mote in the eye of his neighbour.

So we approach the Jewish home we are to visit, the Jewishness of which we may recognise even before we cross its threshold. For there, fixed to the right-hand door-post at about the eye level of a normal adult is one of the most important of all Jewish symbols: a *Mezuzah*, a Hebrew word meaning a door-post.

A door-post on a door-post! How come? The answer is simple. It is a perfect example of a kind of symbolic shorthand. The *Mezuzah* itself, which may be of wood, metal or ivory, and about six inches in length is made to contain a small scroll of parchment on which is written the foundation passage of all Jewish belief and practice: 'Hear, O Israel, the Lord our God, the Lord is one' (Deuteronomy 6:4-9).

Known from the opening word in Hebrew as the *Shema* (hear) it affirms in the simplest terms the absolute unity of God, defines man's duty to God in terms of total love ('with all thy heart, with all thy soul and with all thy might'... and note, it is the individual who is addressed; there is no alibi in this command) bids him teach these words 'diligently' to his children and himself to reflect upon them at all times and in all places, and ends by instructing him to write them on the door-posts of his house and on his gates.

But since gates and door-posts do not afford ideal surfaces upon which to write so many words, some alternative had to be found. The *Mezuzah* was the result. It has an additional feature. Through a small hole, sited with great precision, may be seen one word written on the reverse of the small parchment scroll. It is the word *Shaddai* (Almighty), the name by which, it is said, God made himself known to Abraham (Genesis 17:1).

Nothing could be simpler, more practical or more reassuring. Every time he leaves his home or returns to it the Jew is reminded of the essence of his faith, and the ultimate sanction for his whole way of life: the unity and the omnipotence of his God. Small wonder that the devout Jew as he passed the *Mezuzah* grew into the habit of touching it with his fingers with which he then touched his lips. The Psalmist's exultant outburst: 'Oh, how I love thy law' was no exaggeration. He really did.

There was only one thing more. A man could not so love his God as he was bidden by the words of the *Shema* and not love His creation also, including his neighbour; however difficult and tiresome the neighbour might prove himself to be. The inescapable corollary of the command to love the Lord his God with the whole of his being was the bidding to love his neighbour as himself (Leviticus 19:18).

Thus, on the very threshold of the Jewish home, we find an impressively comprehensive programme for living. 'The words which I command thee this day' have always been understood as embracing the whole of the 'Mosaic code', which, directly or by implication cover pretty well every aspect of a man's life in terms of his relation not only to his God but also to his fellow man. Apart from the writer of the 119th Psalm no one perhaps has better expressed what all this is about than Horatius Bonar, a Scottish divine and hymn writer of the nineteenth century who wrote in one of his best known hymns:

25

> So shall no part of day or night
> From sacredness be free,
> But all my life in every step
> Be fellowship with Thee.

The fixing of the *Mezuzah* whenever a Jewish family moves into a new home is, not surprisingly, the occasion for a service of consecration, performed by the Rabbi, and attended by all the members of the family and their friends. It begins naturally with a blessing (there is a blessing for every conceivable occasion, whether sad or happy, in Jewish life):

> Blessed art Thou, O Lord our God,
> King of the universe,
> Who hast hallowed us by thy commandments,
> And commanded us to affix the Mezuzah.

This is followed by the recitation of Psalm 30, which is said to have been used at the dedication of the second Temple in Jerusalem, Psalm 15, which summarises the Jewish ideal for human conduct, and, for obvious reasons, Psalm 127:

> Unless the Lord builds the house,
> its builders will have toiled in vain.
> Unless the Lord keeps watch over a city,
> in vain the watchman stands on guard.

There follow also some verses from the longest of all Psalms, the 119th, an acrostic Psalm in which each of the twenty-two sections, each of eight verses, begins with successive letters of the Hebrew alphabet. The particular verses selected for this occasion are taken from the four sections whose initial letters, BRKH, spell the Hebrew word for blessing. The sections are those beginning with verses 9, 153, 81 and 33. Of those that are read from the first section a former Chief Rabbi, Dr J.H. Hertz, wrote that 'they overflow with passionate love of the Divine commandments

which are hailed as the safeguard and the joy of life'
(*Commentary on the Daily Prayer Book*, p.1021).

The service ends with the offering of prayers of which
the following might well be shared by every Christian
who seeks the blessing of God upon his home and
family life:

> Bestow thy blessings upon the master of this house.
> Bless, O Lord, his substance and accept the work of his hands.
> Keep him far from sin and transgressing.
> Let thy grace be upon him,
> And prosper thou his labours and undertakings.
>
> May thy loving kindness
> Be with her who looketh well to the ways of her household,
> And may she be mindful that the woman who feareth the Lord,
> She shall be praised.
>
> Bestow upon their sons and daughters
> The spirit of wisdom and understanding.
> Lead them in the path of thy commandments,
> So that all who see them may acknowledge
> That they are an offspring blessed of the Lord,
> Blessed with a knowledge of the Law and with the fear of thee.
>
> Preserve them from all evil;
> Preserve their lives.
> May thy gracious promise be realised in them;
> Blessed shalt thou be when thou comest in,
> Blessed when thou goest out. it.
>
> And even as we have been permitted to consecrate this house,
> So grant that we may together witness
> The dedication of thy great and holy temple in Jerusalem,
> Speedily in our days. Amen.

Now we are ready to cross the threshold to see for
ourselves a host of other symbolic objects and many
symbolic acts, all calculated to remind the Jew that
he is a citizen of two worlds: an earthly and a heavenly. For Judaism knows no total separation between
the sacred and the secular, between earth and heaven.

Gates of Heaven

I—The Home

Home as a gate of heaven! A fanciful idea? Perhaps. And yet, I wonder. Perhaps it has something to do with a childhood recollection of singing a Sunday-School hymn which did its best to persuade us by frequent repetition of the line: 'Heaven is my home' that there was little point in hoping for very much in the way of happiness here on earth. Not that we took it all that seriously, but I cannot help feeling that challenged by that rather melancholy reflection some of my Jewish friends might have transposed the line and sung: 'Home is my heaven'.

Not that every Jewish home of course merits that description. Jews are no more exempt from family quarrels than the rest of us. That is a fact they have never tried to conceal from the earliest days of their history. Jacob, for example, was to become one of the greatest of the Patriarchs yet he deprived his twin brother Esau of his birthright by deceiving their father with the help of their mother. In the loneliness of a night spent under the stars, as a fugitive from the home he had broken by his deception, with only a stone for a pillow, Jacob was to discover that the place where he lay could be 'no other than the house of God and very gate of heaven'. But the story does not end there. For Jacob himself was to live to establish a home and to bring up a family which, for all its problems, was to live as near to the 'gate of heaven' as he had found himself to be on that solitary night under the stars near Bethel.

The ideal time to visit a Jewish home is of course a Friday evening, when the whole family, fresh from the labours of another week, gather to welcome the coming of the Sabbath. It is a magic hour of which a nineteenth century German-Jewish writer said that it 'planted a heaven in every Jewish home, filling it with long-expected and wishfully-greeted peace, making each home a sanctuary, the father a priest, the mother who lights the Sabbath candles an angel of light.' (B. Jacob quoted by J.H. Hertz: *Commentary on Pentateuch*, p.298).

The first and overwhelming impression the visitor receives on entering the home on Friday evening is of tidiness and good order. The table is covered with a spotlessly clean white cloth. It is adorned with two candle sticks, the most beautiful the family possess, whose two candles await the kindling which marks the inauguration of the Sabbath. Concealed under an embroidered cover are two loaves, usually of plaited bread, recalling the double portion of manna the Israelites were commanded to collect on the eve of the Sabbath as they journeyed through the wilderness. A goblet or chalice and a bottle of wine with which to sanctify the Sabbath complete the ritual furnishing of the table.

The father of the family and the older children, together with other members of the community, greet the coming of the Sabbath in the Synagogue, while the mother, the 'angel of light', stays at home to complete the preparation of the meal. At the appropriate moment she will kindle the Sabbath lights greeting the coming of the Sabbath with a meditation which might be any mother's prayer:

Lord of the Universe
I am about to perform the sacred duty
Of kindling the lights in honour of the Sabbath,
Even as it is written:
And thou shalt call the Sabbath a delight,
And the holy day of the Lord honourable.
And may the effect of my fulfilling this commandment be
That the stream of abundant life and heavenly blessing
Flow in upon me and mine;
That thou be gracious unto us,
And cause thy presence to dwell among us.
Father of Mercy
O continue thy loving kindness
Unto me and unto my dear ones.
Make me worthy
To (rear my children so that they)
Walk in the way of the righteous before thee,
Loyal to thy Law and clinging to good deeds.
Keep thou far from us
All manner of shame, grief and care;
And grant that peace, light and joy
Ever abide in our home.
For with thee is the fountain of life;
In thy light do we see light. Amen.

On their return from the Synagogue it is customary for the father to bless his children. Placing his hands on the head of each in turn he recites the Aaronic blessing (Numbers 6:24-26), prefacing this in the case of the boys with the words: 'God make thee as Ephraim and Manasseh' (the two sons of Joseph upon whom their grandfather Jacob bestowed his special blessing and of whom tradition has it that they voluntarily gave up their place in the Egyptian aristocracy rather than deny their Jewishness), and in the case of the girls: 'God make thee as Sarah, Rebekah, Rachel and Leah' (the wives of the three great patriarchs).

He then acknowledges the central place of the mother in the home and the family by reciting the concluding verses of the book of Proverbs (31:10-31): an acrostic poem which extols the virtues of what the New English Bible translates as a 'capable' and the Jerusalem Bible as a 'perfect' wife.

And so we come to the table for the meal itself, the highlight of the week for every Jewish family. However simple it will be the best the mother can provide. It begins with the *kiddush*, a simple service for the sanctification of this holiday. Recalling that 'on the seventh day [of creation] God had finished his work which he had made, and he rested... and blessed and hallowed the seventh day because he rested on it from all his work...' (Genesis 2:1-3), the father pours out a cup of wine with the words: 'Blessed are thou, O Lord our God King of the Universe who created the fruit of the vine'. Then, having drunk from it himself, he passes it to his wife and so to all who sit at table with them.

This is followed by the uncovering and blessing of the bread with the words: 'Blessed art thou, O Lord our God, King of the Universe, who bringest forth bread from the earth'. The bread is then broken and shared with all at the table: a simple observance of deep significance and great antiquity in which the Christian guest will surely recognise the prototype of what through the voice and hands of Jesus of Nazareth was to become the sacrament of Holy Communion.

And because bread is a basic constituent of every meal, while wine is reserved for the more festive occasion, this simple blessing of the bread, the recitation of which takes as little as five seconds, has become the traditional form of 'grace' to be said before every meal. It is only when the meal is ended that there is time to relax and rejoice for a while in the contemplation of the goodness of God 'of whose bounty we have partaken'. The traditional 'grace' which follows the meal is, in fact, a short service in which all the participants share, singing together a number of prayers and scriptural passages woven together into a pattern of joyous devotion. Parts of the grace are traceable as far back as the second century of the current era. The whole reflects unbounded confidence in the:

> Lord our God, King of the universe, O God our Father, our King, our Mighty one, the Holy One of Jacob, our Shepherd, the Shepherd of Israel, O King who art kind and dealest kindly with all.

In this, as in so many other ways, that shrewd combination of sanctity and common sense which characterises so much of Jewish 'religious' life finds its perfect expression.

The Sabbath evening meal traditionally had one other delightful feature: the communal singing of table songs which, as Israel Zangwill once wrote, sum up 'in light and jingling metre, the very essence of holy joyousness—neither riotous nor ascetic: the note of spiritualised common sense which has been the keynote of historical Judaism'.

One of the best known of these songs dates back to the twelfth century and was composed by Abraham ibn Ezra, who lived in Spain from 1092 to 1167. In addition to his skill as a poet he was a distinguished scholar, philosopher and traveller. He visited England in 1158 where he wrote a famous *Epistle on the Sabbath*:

> If we the Sabbath keep with faithful heart,
> The Lord will Israel keep with love divine;
> Of his good grace and our true loyalty,
> O let this day for ever prove the sign!
>
> The daily round its restless turmoil ends,
> Our ears are closed to worldly battle-cries;
> From toil set free, the hour we dedicate
> To ponder on the Law that maketh wise.
>
> > If we the Sabbath...
>
> The wondrous memories refresh our soul,
> Of manna, on our sires conferred of yore;
> For us, as for our fathers, Heaven provides
> A double portion of the Sabbath store.
>
> > If we the Sabbath...
>
> O honoured day, that sets our heart aglow!
> A day of joy, ordained to make us glad!
> With bread and wine we greet thee and good cheer,
> A traitor he, whose Sabbath heart is sad!
>
> > If we the Sabbath...

Throughout the evening, whether at prayer, eating, singing or simply engaging in conversation, the men and boys will have kept their heads covered. We shall find the same in the Synagogue. Indeed there are some very orthodox Jews who wear some form of head-covering, be it only the simplest of skull caps, at all times and in all places. If we ask why we may well be told in the words of Tevye the Milkman in *The Fiddler on the Roof*: 'It is a tradition: and if you ask me why, I'll tell you: I don't know'.

Not all however have been content with so evasive an answer. In his fascinating study of *Jewish Life in the Middle Ages* (p.300f.), Dr Israel Abrahams wrote: 'anciently, the habit was at most a piece of occasional etiquette, though it afterwards became a strict and general ritual ordinance'. How the transition from 'occasional etiquette' to 'ritual ordinance' took place is not clear, though there are hints here and there. Saint Paul's first letter to the Corinthians (11:4) suggests that it was not customary in his day for the Jews to pray with the head covered. On the other hand, an early rabbinic commentary on Leviticus argues that whereas a man might well stand before an early king 'with head uncovered, trembling with fear and anxiety', God does not require such marks of servitude from his children even when they recite their most solemn prayer. To keep the head covered might thus be interpreted as a privilege, suggesting that 'the respect a Jew had to his God was the reverence of a free man'. In the twelfth and thirteenth centuries there were some who said one thing and some another, until eventually 'the idea became fixed in Jewish minds that to pray bare-headed belongs to those "customs of the Gentiles" which must not be imitated'.

One thing is certain. Whatever the origin of the custom, and however varied the observance has been down through the centuries, the current practice is universally interpreted as a mark of respect and a symbol of acceptance of the principle of the sacredness of all life.

The following morning (Sabbath) it is customary for the whole of the family to go together to the Synagogue: of which more presently. The afternoon provides an opportunity for re-reading, at home or in the Synagogue (sometimes referred to as the 'house of study'), of the weekly passage of the *Torah* and the discussion of some of its finer points. During the summer, with its longer, brighter days, it was also customary to study one of the best known Rabbinical books: *The Ethics of the Fathers* which dates back almost certainly to the time of Jesus. Some of its teachings, many of which were associated with two great Rabbis, Hillel and Shammai, who were contemporaries of his, are couched in short, pithy sayings, easy to remember and inexhaustible in their implications.

Thus, for example, Hillel used to say:

> Judge not thy fellow-man until thou art come into his place; and say not anything which cannot be understood at once in the hope that it will be understood in the end; neither say: When I have leisure I will study; perchance thou wilt have no leisure.

He also used to say:

> If I am not for myself, who will be for me? And if I am only for myself, what am I? And if not now, when?

Anyone who feels tempted to dismiss this either as a glimpse of the obvious, or an example of not very well disguised self-interest will do well to pause and think again. 'Had Hillel left us but this single saying', wrote a nineteenth-century German historian, Ewald, 'we should be for ever grateful to him; for scarce anything can be said more briefly, more profoundly and more earnestly'.

At sunset on Sabbath there occurs another very simple and beautiful home ceremony to mark the beginning of another week. As the inauguration of the Sabbath was marked by the kindling of lights, so at its conclusion a light is extinguished as a symbol of the *Havdalah* or 'separation' between the Sabbath and the rest of the week.

Again a blessing is said, this time over a cup of wine

and a lighted plaited taper. A spice box containing a mixture of sweet-smelling spices is passed round, so that each member of the family may savour again the fragrance of the Sabbath joy and peace. A number of Biblical verses are read and finally the taper is extinguished by dousing it in a saucer of wine. The Sabbath is ended, and a prayer which any Christian might gladly share with his Jewish neighbour, is recited to mark the beginning of another week:

Sovereign of the Universe,
Father of mercy and forgiveness,
Grant that we begin the working days
Which are drawing nigh unto us, in peace;
Freed from all sin and transgression;
Cleansed from all iniquity, trespass and wickedness;
And clinging to the study of thy Teaching,
And to the performance of good deeds.

Cause us to hear in the coming week
Tidings of joy and gladness.
May there not arise in the heart of any man envy of us,
Nor in us envy of any man.
O, our King, our God, Father of mercy.
Bless and prosper the work of our hands.

And all who cherish towards us and thy people Israel
Thoughts of good, strengthen and prosper them,
and fulfil their purpose;
But all who devise against us and thy people Israel,
Plans which are not for our good, O frustrate them
And make their design of none effect;
As it is said,
Take counsel together, and it shall be brought to nought;
Speak the word, and it shall not stand;
For God is with us.

Open unto us, Father of mercies and Lord of forgiveness
In this week and in the week to come,
The gates of light and blessing,
Of redemption and salvation,
Of heavenly help and rejoicing,
Of holiness and peace,
Of the study of thy Torah and of prayer.

In us also let the Scripture be fulfilled:
How beautiful upon the mountains
Are the feet of him that bringeth good tidings,
That announceth peace,

The harbinger of good tidings,
That announceth salvation;
That saith unto Zion,
Thy God reigneth! Amen.

A most important feature of any home, Jewish or non-Jewish, is of course the kitchen. Indeed I never feel a visit to any home is complete which does not include at least a glimpse into the kitchen. On Sabbath, however, the Jewish kitchen is virtually 'closed to visitors'. This is because in the orthodox home, the preparation of all the meals for this 'day of light and rejoicing' on which all manner of 'work' is forbidden is completed before the Sabbath comes in.

The Jewish kitchen, however, is a place of special importance. Jews, even the poorest among them, attach great importance to food; not simply because it is necessary to life, but because the preparation and consumption of every meal has a deeper meaning. It is an acknowledgment both of man's dependence upon God and of his relationship with his fellow-men. It is, as Lion Roth once described it, a form of 'pot-and-pantheism' (*Judaism a Portrait*, p.28).

There are dietary laws which govern not only the kind of foods that may be eaten but also the ways in which they are to be prepared. That these laws should give rise to all kinds of problems is in no way surprising. Some of these were matters of dispute between Jesus and some of his fellow teachers. The earliest Christians were soon wrestling with problems of ritually 'clean' and 'unclean' food, and whether they might eat together with Gentiles or not. The observant twentieth-century Jew still has his problems, particularly over the question of sharing in meals not prepared in accordance with the dietary laws. It was a matter of unusual interest and importance that when in the spring of 1975 the British Chief Rabbi and his wife were entertained by Her Majesty the Queen at Windsor Castle, arrangements were made to bring into the Castle food specially prepared in accordance with these same dietary laws.

What then are these laws? First there are certain foods which are entirely forbidden. Details of these are to be found in Leviticus 11, together with a statement of the ultimate reason and authority for them in verse 45: 'For I am the Lord that brought you out of the land of Egypt to be your God; ye shall therefore be holy, for I am holy'. For the orthodox Jew the authority is beyond question. These 'laws' are accepted as belonging to a category of 'statutes' which do not have to be explained, nor may they be questioned.

Secondly, meat is permitted only if it has been slaughtered in such a way as to ensure that every drop of blood is drained from the flesh before it is cooked. This practice derives from the Biblical prohibition against consuming blood: 'For the blood is the life; and thou shall not eat the life with the flesh' (Deuteronomy 12:23). The method of slaughter practised to ensure instantaneous death and the quickest possible draining of blood from the carcass is known as *shechitah*. This practice involves the cutting of the animal's throat with a blade honed to perfect sharpness. It has been widely attacked on grounds of alleged cruelty.

Veterinary experts however have shown that it is at least as humane as any other method of animal slaughter and more so than most. It is practised only by most highly trained and skilled slaughterers whose work is subject to all the moral and ethical sanctions imposed by the *Torah*.

Finally it is forbidden to mix milk and meat foods. This prohibition stems from the Biblical ban on 'seething a kid in its mother's milk' (Exodus 23:19; Exodus 34:26; Deuteronomy 14:21). The practical implications of this seemingly strange command are legion. One could not, for example, consume any form of milk food (butter, cheese, cream, milk, either by themselves or in combination with any other food, e.g. fruit and cream, coffee and cream, bread and cheese) within a specified number of hours of consuming any kind of meat, either alone or in combination with other foods. No reason is given for this command which is accepted by the orthodox as one of the statutes to be obeyed without question. Others have sought to explain it on health grounds.

Meticulous observance of this prohibition requires that milk dishes shall never be served upon plates or dishes that have been used for meat in any form. In the strictly orthodox home therefore it is customary to have two completely separate sets of pots, pans, crockery and cutlery together with two sinks or two bowls for washing-up purposes. All of which, of course, can very easily become very tiresome and very difficult to observe when meals must be consumed in hotels and restaurants where such requirements are not even known let alone understood and observed.

The kitchen then, and all that happens in it and flows from it, is of the greatest importance in the life of the family and the community, and the visitor to the Jewish home may well reflect upon some words of Dr J.H. Hertz who wrote:

> The ancient gibe, revived in modern days and used as the final argument against the dietary laws is: 'Not what goes into the mouth but what comes out of it, defileth man'. Now, the State could never endorse the literal meaning of the words: 'Not what goes into the mouth defileth a man'. It holds that poison which goes into the mouth *does* defile, and classes poisoning as a peculiarly detestable kind of murder. Likewise Science sets its face against unripe fruit, adulterated milk, diseased meat—things that go into the mouth... and as to the words 'only that which comes out of the mouth defileth man', one needs but to recall the fact that *out of* the mouth comes speech which raises man above the brute, prayer that unites man to his Creator, words of cheer and faith spoken to the sorrow laden.

From the Sabbath, via the kitchen, we come finally to the simple symbols and acts which mark the daily devotion of the Jew: his morning and evening prayers and the ritual observances that accompany some of them.

It is no doubt a relic of a patriarchal system that requires the devout Jew every morning to thank his God that he did not make him a woman, while his wife modestly blesses the Lord, her God, the King of the universe, that he made her according to his will. It would, however, be a very serious mistake to imagine that Jewish men have always regarded themselves as superior beings, or for that matter that Jewish women have felt themselves either to be or to be thought to be inferior. The Jewish way of life, though theoretically patriarchal, was in essence very much more a matriarchy. The role of the housewife and mother has always been seen and accepted by all the family as the fulfilment of a divine vocation. She did not need, as did her husband, outward symbols to remind her of her religious duties. To run a Jewish home, to give birth to a Jewish child, to raise a Jewish family: these were for her a form, not of domestic slavery, but of complete fulfilment.

The husband's religious observances were much more formal, though basically very simple and very rich in meaning. One of the earliest prayers at the beginning of the day says quite simply:

> Blessed art thou, O Lord our God, King of the universe
> Who has hallowed us by thy commandments
> And given us command concerning the washing of hands.

This is followed by a further blessing of God:

> Who has formed man in wisdom
> And created in him many passages and vessels.
> It is well known before thy glorious throne
> That if but one of these be opened
> Or one of these be closed
> It would be impossible to exist and stand before Thee

> Blessed are thou, O Lord,
> Who art the wondrous healer of all flesh.

From cleanliness of body, which in Jewish life is not merely 'next to Godliness' but part of it, the third 'blessing' of the day focuses upon the chief end of living which is 'to occupy ourselves with the words of *Torah*':

> Blessed art thou, O Lord our God, King of the universe
> Who has hallowed us by thy commandments
> And commanded us to occupy ourselves with the words of Torah.

And that is an all-embracing command. What the Gospel is to the Christian the *Torah* is to the Jew, for whom the 'words of *Torah*' are uniquely set out in the first five books of the Hebrew Bible, the Pentateuch, the five books of Moses, or the Law as they are variously called. All the rest, the Prophets, the other canonical writings and the teachings of the Rabbis are but an extension, and interpretation, a commentary on the *Torah* to be 'read, marked, learned, and inwardly digested' and then embodied in the whole of a man's life, wherever he is and whatever he may be doing.

There are petitions too, and the recitation of certain passages from the teachings of the Rabbis which link general principles with particular applications and the life of this world with that of the world to come. And all this is embellished with the use of the *tallith*, or prayer shawl, and *tefillin*, or phylacteries: symbols of great antiquity and rich in meaning.

The *tallith*, a Hebrew word meaning 'garment' or 'cloak', is a kind of glorified scarf, with a silken fringe at each end. As he puts it on the wearer recites the following prayer:

> I am here enwrapping myself in this fringed robe, in fulfilment of the command of my Creator, as it is written in the *Torah*: They shall make them a fringe upon the corners of their garments throughout their generations. And even as I cover myself with the *tallith* in this world, so may my soul deserve to be clothed with a beauteous spiritual robe in the world to come, in the garden of Eden. Amen.

Similarly with the *tefillin*. The Hebrew word means literally 'prayers'. The Greek 'phylactery', which has been universally adopted as the anglicised equivalent, most inappropriately means 'amulet'. The *tefillin*, of which there are always two, are in no measure a 'charm against evil'. They are small cube-shaped leather boxes attached to long straps: one for the head, to emphasise the importance of the mind, and one for the left arm as being near to the heart or the seat of the emotions. Each contains, in minute separate compartments, four tiny strips of parchment on which are written four passages of Scripture: Exodus 13:1-10; 11:16; Deuteronomy 6:4-9; 11:13-21. Their purpose is recalled as the wearer binds them to his arm and forehead reciting as he does:

> I am now intent upon the act of putting on the *tefillin*, in fulfilment of the command of my Creator, who hath commanded us to lay the *tefillin*, as it is written in the *Torah*: And thou shalt bind them for a sign upon thine hand, and they shall be for frontlets between thine eyes. Within these *tefillin* are placed four sections of the *Torah*, that declare the absolute unity of God, and remind us of the miracles and wonders which he wrought for us when he brought us forth from Egypt, even he who hath power over the highest and the lowest to deal with them according to his will. He hath commanded us to lay the *tefillin* upon the hand as a memorial of his outstretched arm; opposite the heart, to indicate the duty of subjecting the longings and designs of our heart to his service, blessed be he; and upon the head over against the brain, thereby teaching that the mind, whose seat is in the brain, together with all senses and faculties, is to be subjected to his service, blessed be he. May the effect of the precept thus observed be to extend to me long life with sacred influences and holy thoughts, free from every approach, even in imagination, to sin and iniquity. May the evil inclination not mislead or entice us, but may we be led to serve the Lord as it is in our hearts to do. Amen.

Finally, as at the beginning of the day, there are prayers also to be said before retiring to rest. In certain traditions these begin with the words:

> Master of the universe,
> Behold,
> I forgive every one who has injured me,
> And may no one be punished
> Because of his wrong to me.

This is followed by a prayer which again any Christian might be glad to use, beginning again with the now familiar blessing:

Blessed art thou, O Lord our God, King of the universe,
Who makest the bands of sleep to fall upon mine eyes,
And slumber upon mine eyelids.

May it be thy will, O Lord my God and God of my fathers,
to suffer me to lie down in peace
and to let me rise up again in peace.

Let not my thoughts trouble me,
Nor evil dreams, nor evil fancies,
But let my rest be perfect before thee.

O lighten mine eyes, lest I sleep the sleep of death
For it is thou who givest light to the apple of the eye.
Blessed art thou, O Lord,
Who givest light to the whole world in thy glory.

The *Shema* follows, together with the 91st Psalm,
several other passages of Scripture and, repeated
three times, the fifth verse of Psalm 4:

Stand in awe and sin not:
Commune with your own heart upon your bed,
And be still.

And finally one of the greatest hymns of a not very
extensive Jewish hymnology. Attributed to Salomon
ibn Gabirol, a great philosopher and poet in eleventh-
century Spain, this short hymn *Adon Olam* (Lord of
the World) ends with a verse with which, again, anyone at the end of a tiring day might happily lay his
head upon his pillow:

I place my soul within his palm
Before I sleep as when I wake,
And though my body I forsake,
Rest in the Lord in fearless calm.

In some degree, of course, this picture of the Jewish
home is an idealised one. It is true, of course, that in
today's world gateways to heaven are all too easily
blocked with a host of extraneous things: the sheer
pressures of contemporary urban life, the eroding influence of new ways of thought, of new and as yet un-

digested experiences and the all-pervasive influence of the mass media. But that is not the whole story. For the gates of heaven are never blocked on the other side. The spirit of God is free and unconfined and is forever breaking through in the hour of man's deepest need.

Gates of Heaven

II—The Synagogue

The Jewish home and the synagogue have always been very near neighbours. Spiritually the one is simply an extension of the other. Just as in the home all the members of the family meet together, so in the synagogue the families themselves assemble to pray, to study and to engage in a wide range of communal activities.

Else what is a synagogue for? The name itself is Greek and means quite simply 'to come together'. It is a translation of the Hebrew word for congregation or assembly. Although no one knows for certain when the synagogue first emerged, there is general agreement that its roots go back as far as the Babylonian exile in the sixth century B.C. where the exiles, finding it difficult 'to sing the Lord's song in a strange land' (Psalm 137:4), used to gather in small groups to pray and study together.

Later, with the dispersion of the Jews throughout the Graeco-Roman world and the destruction of the Temple in 70 A.D., the synagogue became quite naturally the central focus of Jewish life, thought and worship. The building itself might be small or large. It is said that there was one in Alexandria so large that it was necessary to have men with flags stationed at strategic points to enable the congregation to keep in touch with the progress of the service. Traditionally, and for a variety of reasons, mainly economic, the preference has been for small rather than large. For many congregations a converted house, or even a room in a house, had of necessity to suffice. Not surprisingly, therefore, few regulations were laid down concerning the overall appearance. Where a congregation was wealthy enough to enjoy the luxury of a purpose-built synagogue its design would normally reflect the architectural patterns of the environment, though a too close approximation to a recognisable ecclesiastical pattern was obviously avoided.

There were, however, certain basic requirements. A window or windows, for example. And that for reasons over and above the obvious need for light. One was to preserve the tradition associated with Daniel who (6:10) 'had windows made in his roof-chamber looking towards Jerusalem' so that he could offer prayers and praises to God three times a day 'as his custom had always been'.

Once inside, the principal features of the synagogue are quickly apparent. On the eastern wall, since synagogues like churches (in the west) are orientated towards Jerusalem, is the Ark. This is a cupboard, in which are kept the scrolls of the *Torah*. It is normally covered by a curtain which, like the Ark itself, will vary in size and splendour according to the wealth of the congregation. Some of the curtains, normally of velvet, are heavily and richly embroidered with silver or gold thread.

In the centre of the synagogue built on traditional lines is a platform (*bimah*) from which the prayers are read (or chanted) by the cantor who stands always facing the Ark; and to which the scrolls are carried in solemn procession from the Ark for the reading of the weekly portion during the Sabbath morning service. In the modern synagogue, particularly of the progressive Jews, the *bimah* has given way to a lectern and pulpit facing the congregation.

Above the Ark burns a perpetual light (*ner tamid*) symbolising the divine presence, the direct link with the tabernacle and the Temple and the prototype of the light which burns before the reserved sacrament in the Catholic Church. The Ark itself is adorned with a symbolic replica of the two tablets of the law on which each of the ten commandments is represented by its initial letter in Hebrew. Other forms of ornamentation vary according to the wealth of the congregation. In some synagogues there are stained-glass windows, frequently illustrating the major festivals.

In all synagogues, of whatever section of the community, the seats are so arranged that the worshippers can always look towards the Ark. In the traditional orthodox synagogue the women sit apart from the men, normally in a gallery specially reserved for them.

So much for the setting. Whether the synagogue be large or small, simple or ornate, however, the pattern of worship is everywhere broadly the same. Basically, in orthodox synagogues throughout the world the service is conducted in Hebrew. This means that the Jew who really knows his prayer-book will quickly feel at home in any synagogue anywhere.

On Sabbath the daily services of morning and evening prayer, the precursors of the Christian matins and evensong, are augmented by a special service for the reading of the *Torah* which, together with the normal morning service, may last for anything up to three or three-and-a-half hours.

Not surprisingly, perhaps, the pattern is modified in progressive synagogues in two important respects: the service itself is considerably shortened, and much greater use is made of the vernacular, though Hebrew still plays an important part.

In all types of synagogue the service is sung or chanted. In the orthodox synagogue the singing is without instrumental accompaniment. The 'reader' (*chazan*) acts as precentor, and is normally assisted by a choir. Only for weddings may an instrument (usually a portable harmonium) be brought into the orthodox synagogue, not to provide an accompaniment to the singing, of which in the brief marriage service there is very little, but to ensure that the bride and bridegroom are able to leave to the accompaniment of one of the conventional wedding marches.

Before any statutory service can take place there must be a quorum (*minyan*) of ten adult males, where adult means anyone who has been confirmed (*bar mitzvah*) or initiated into full membership of the community. This normally takes place at the age of twelve or thirteen. So important, indeed, is the *minyan* that while no service can take place without it, where ten men are together assembled neither a rabbi nor any other official is needed to make the service valid, nor is it necessary that the prayers should be said in the synagogue.

So, at last, we come to the service itself, and as first-time visitors the most obvious service to attend would be that for the Sabbath morning. The rabbi or any member of the congregation would almost certainly suggest that we arrive in time for the special service for the reading of the *Torah*. But since we are visitors in imagination only we shall arrive in time for the beginning of the earlier service.

On arriving at the synagogue men, if they are without a head-covering of their own, will normally be provided with a paper skull-cap. If their visit is expected they will almost certainly be introduced to a member of the congregation who will sit with them and with the aid of a prayer-book and a copy of the pentateuch will guide them through the service. They will be particularly fortunate if these two volumes happen to be those annotated by Dr J.H. Hertz.

On entering the synagogue the worshipper repeats to himself the following verses culled from Numbers 24:5 and Psalms 5:8, 26:8 and 69:14; verses which when the service commences are taken up and sung by the whole congregation:

> How goodly are thy tents, O Jacob,
>   Thy dwelling places, O Israel.
> As for me, in the abundance of thy loving kindness
>   Will I come into thy house.
> I will worship towards thy holy Temple
>   In the fear of thee.
> Lord, I love the habitation of thy house
>   And the place where thy glory dwelleth.
> I will worship and bow down,
>   I will bend the knee before the Lord my healer.
> May my prayer before thee, O Lord,
>   Be in acceptable time.
> O God, in the abundance of thy loving kindness,
>   Answer me with thy sure salvation.

This is followed by the singing of one of the best known hymns of the synagogue. Written by a Rabbi in Rome early in the fourteenth century it is based upon a formulation of the thirteen basic principles of the Jewish faith made by one of the most famous Rabbis of all time: Moses Maimonides, in twelfth-century Spain. Though in no way comparable in authority or usage with the Apostles' or Nicene Creeds in Christendom, this formulation provides the most widely accepted statement of the principles (Jews do not take kindly to the word doctrine) of Judaism.

The hymn is sung to a melody well-known in Church circles as the tune to 'The God of Abraham praise'. This is hardly surprising for the composer of the hymn, Thomas Olivers, one of John Wesley's preachers, wrote his verses after attending a service in the Great Synagogue in Duke's Place in the East End of London. He called on Leoni, the cantor a day or so later and asked permission to use the melody to which he there and then gave the name 'Leoni', by which it is still known in Church hymn-books. In addition to the familiar 'God of Abraham praise' the Methodist hymn-book of 1933 also contains a paraphrase of some of the verses of the original Jewish hymn:

> Praise to the living God!
>   All praised be His name,
> Who was, and is, and is to be,
>   For aye the same!
> The One Eternal God
>   Ere aught that now appears:
> The First, the Last, beyond all thought
>   His timeless years!

To many Christians today it is surprising to learn that Jews believe, as their fathers have done since long before the coming of Christ, in the resurrection of the dead. This belief was expressed by Maimonides in the thirteenth of his principles:

> I believe with perfect faith that there will be a revival of the dead at the time when it shall please the Creator, blessed be his name, and exalted be his name for ever and ever.

and appears impressively in the concluding verse of this paraphrase, made by a Rabbi, Max Landsberg, in the State of New York early in the nineteenth century:

> Eternal life hath He
>   Implanted in the Soul;
> His love shall be our strength and stay
>   While ages roll.
> Praise to the living God
>   All praised be His name
> Who was, and is and is to be
>   For aye the same.

The hymn is followed by the singing of the following Psalms: 19, 34, 90, 91, 135, 136, 33, 92, 145-150. Here the liturgy of the synagogue differs from those Christian traditions which have incorporated the whole of the Psalter in their worship. Penitence and praise both have their place, but no use is made in the Jewish service of the imprecatory psalms. It is a good pattern and ends appropriately with the whole congregation repeating the concluding verse of the final Psalm: 'Let everything that hath breath praise the Lord: Hallelujah'.

Attention then focuses upon the central affirmation of Judaism: the *Shema*. Two wonderful prayers precede this affirmation. The first praises the Creator who 'every day opens the windows of the East ... giving light to the whole world and to its inhabitants who were created by his attribute of mercy', and goes on to reflect on the wonders of creation, the gift of the Sabbath, and the splendours of the heavenly Kingdom. The second, known, as are so many of the prayers and hymns, by its opening word in Hebrew, as *ahava*: 'thou hast loved' extols the love of God in entrusting to his people 'the statutes of life' and asks that it be put into their hearts 'to understand and to discern, to mark, learn and teach, to heed, to do and to fulfil in love all the words of instruction in thy *Torah*'.

The *Shema*, as we have seen, comprises three passages: Deuteronomy 6:4-9, 11:13-22, and Numbers 15:37-42. This is followed by a prayer recalling the deliverance from Egypt, which evoked a response of 'hymns, songs, praises, blessing and thanksgivings to the King, the living and ever-enduring God, who is high and exalted and who raises up the lonely, frees the prisoners, delivers the meek, helps the poor and answers his people when they cry to him'.

Then comes the most solemn prayer of all. It is sometimes referred to as *the* prayer (*tefillah*), sometimes as the eighteen benedictions (*shemoneh esreh*) and, most frequently, as the prayer that is said standing (*amidah*). One of the oldest prayers in the liturgy, it reached its present form round about the end of the first century A.D. Normally it comprises a series of benedictions: three containing acts of praise, twelve of petition and three of thanksgiving. Its solemnity is emphasised by the fact that it is twice repeated: the first time in a silence that can be felt. Beginning with the familiar words from Psalm 51:15:

> O Lord, open thou my lips
> And my mouth shall show forth thy praise

it goes on to reflect upon the whole process of history from the call of Abraham to the long-anticipated coming of the Messiah:

> Blessed art thou, O Lord our God and God of our fathers,
> God of Abraham, God of Isaac and God of Jacob,
> The great, mighty and revered God, the most high God,
> Who bestowest loving kindness and possessest all things;
> Who rememberest the pious deeds of the patriarchs,
> And in love will bring a redeemer
> To their children's children
> For thy name's sake.

In this act of silent meditation the worshipper stands in the presence of God not simply as a member of a community, but momentarily and essentially as an individual. Even so, his first thought is not for his physical or material needs but for understanding, repentance and forgiveness. Only when he has sought these blessings does he go on to pray for deliverance from affliction, for healing, and for the fruits of the earth. Then, resuming his place as a member of the beloved community he goes on to pray for the reunion of its scattered members, for the restoration of the regime of righteousness, for the re-building of Jerusalem and the coming of the Messianic age.

The whole is rounded off with an act of thanksgiving and a brief pause for private prayer: a pause which has given birth over the centuries to many gems of devotion, some of which are quoted by Dr Hertz in his Commentary on the Prayer Book and one of the loveliest of which might well find a place in any contemporary anthology of prayer:

> May it be thy will, O Lord, our God, to cause love and brotherhood, peace and comradeship, to abide in our lot; to enlarge our border with disciples, to prosper our goal with happy endings and fulfilment of hope. May we be of those who have a portion in

the life to come. Strengthen us with good companionship and fortify our good impulses in this life; so that the reverence of Thy name be ever the longing of our heart. And may this our happiness in reverencing Thee be remembered by Thee for good.

The whole service now reaches its long-anticipated climax in the reading of the Law. In importance, though in no other respect, for Judaism knows nothing of sacramental worship or doctrine, its place may be compared with that of Holy Communion in the life of the Church. Everything leads up to it. Everything flows from it. Of the Law itself one of the early Rabbis once said: 'Turn it over and over. For everything is in it'.

For liturgical purposes the *Torah* has been divided, since the days of the Maccabees, into regular portions for reading on Sabbaths and festivals. Originally based upon a triennial cycle, the portions were relatively short. With the dispersion of the Jews throughout the Graeco-Roman world, however, the triennial gave place to a yearly cycle with consequently longer weekly portions, a practice which has survived until today.

Because these weekly portions run to a considerable length, each is divided into seven sub-sections. And because Judaism is essentially a lay-religion seven members of the congregation are called up to the reading desk, each to be responsible for one of the seven sections. There was a time when each member so called would read the portion himself. No doubt some still could. But the liturgical reading from the Scroll requires special training. Today therefore it is undertaken by the *chazan* who is a highly trained and competent officiant. Here, as in so many aspects of Jewish worship, we find an unbroken link with the Temple in which Priests (*Cohens*) and the Levites played the leading roles which disappeared with the destruction of the Temple and the end of the sacrificial system. Their priority in a no longer existing hierarchy survived, however, in connection with the reading of the Law. Always the first to be called upon is some one whose family name is Cohen and who is therefore believed to be a descendant of the Temple priesthood. The second is always a Levy (or Levite). And since it is regarded as an honour to be called up to the reading it is customary to invite any member of the congregation who is either just about to be or has just been married, one whose wife has just borne him a child, one who is commemorating the anniversary of a parent's death or who has just completed the seven days of mourning for a member of his family. And, of course, a boy who is just becoming *bar mitzvah*.

To become *bar mitzvah* (which means 'a son of the commandment') is the equivalent of confirmation in the Church and one of the most important occasions in the life of every Jew. There is no question of slipping unobtrusively into membership of the community. On this one occasion in his life every Jew is required actually to read the portion of the Law for which he is called up.

'Reading' in this connection in fact is a form of chanting, the performance of which requires very special preparation. The Hebrew text in the actual Scroll is still hand-written on parchment. Moreover, it is written in consonants only as originally were all Hebrew texts. Vowel symbols were invented only in the ninth century A.D., but were not allowed to be written into the text of the Scroll. This ensures that the *bar mitzvah* has really studied at least one portion of the *Torah* which he is unlikely ever to forget. Of one thing, however, he can be sure. Great though he may feel the ordeal to be, no performer could hope for a more sympathetic audience, every member of which after all has himself endured the same gruelling experience.

For the future, all that will be required of him, as of all who are called up to 'read a portion' is that he should say this blessing at the beginning:

> Blessed art thou, O Lord our God, King of the universe
> Who hast chosen us from all peoples
> And hast given us thy Law.
> Blessed art thou, O Lord, who givest the Law.

and at the end:

> Blessed art thou, O Lord our God, King of the universe
> Who hast given us the Law of truth
> And hast planted everlasting life in our midst.
> Blessed art thou, O Lord, who givest the Law.

And because the idea of 'the chosen people' mentioned in the first of these two blessings is so frequent a cause of misunderstanding on the part of Jews and non-Jews alike, it is worth reflecting on the following note by Dr J.H. Hertz in his Commentary on the Prayer Book at this point:

> These simple but sublime words stress the selection of Israel (Exodus 19:5) and the great fact of Revelation. God is the Father of all mankind, but he has chosen Israel to be His in a special degree, not to privilege and rulership, but to be 'a light unto the nations', to proclaim and testify to the spiritual values of life.

The reading from the Law is followed by a 'second lesson' from the prophets. This is known as the *Haftarah* (or conclusion). The prophetic readings also follow a prescribed pattern and are related to the portion from the *Torah* in very much the same way as in the Christian liturgy the Gospel and Epistle for successive Sundays and festivals are linked together. In this connection it is important to remember that the arrangement of the books in the Hebrew Bible differs from that of the Christian version. Thus, for example, Joshua and Judges and the books of Samuel and Kings are included among the Prophets, whereas Daniel is not; a reminder that in the Jewish view the primary function of the prophet is to proclaim the will of God in relation to the situation of his own time, rather than to speculate on the distant future.

This 'prophetic' lesson is always very much shorter than that from the *Torah*. Its average length is twenty-one verses and requires the services of only one reader.

This whole exercise of the reading of the *Torah* and the *Haftarah* is set within a framework of liturgical action broadly reminiscent of the setting for the reading of the Gospel and Epistle in a celebration of Holy Communion. Immediately following upon the *Amidah* prayer the Ark is opened and the Scroll from which the reading is to be made is taken out by the reader who, together with the congregation, sings:

> For out of Zion shall go forth the Law
> And the word of the Lord from Jerusalem.

The *Shema* is again repeated and the Scroll is then carried in solemn procession round the synagogue. Those members of the congregation who are near enough to do so frequently touch the mantle in which the Scroll is 'dressed' with the fringes of their prayer shawl which they then convey to their lips, as an outward and visible sign of deeply felt devotion.

This devotion is further reflected in the ornaments with which the Scroll is bedecked. These are a rich velvet mantle, frequently heavily embroidered with gold or silver thread, a silver shield or breastplate which hangs over the front of the Scroll, and a silver pointer usually in the form of a hand with the index finger extended, which is used by the *chazan* to avoid touching the parchment itself with his own fingers. There are also two silver finials, decorated with bells whose happy tinkling is calculated to inspire the worshippers with the joy of the Lord who has entrusted them with this precious revelation of himself.

The reading is followed by prayers of intercession for the teachers and religious leaders of the community, for the congregation itself, for all who 'give bread to the wayfarers, and charity to the poor, and all such who occupy themselves in faithfulness with the wants of the congregation', and finally for the rulers of the State: in Britain for the Queen and the members of the Royal Family and for all her counsellors that 'in a spirit of wisdom and understanding ... they may uphold the peace of the realm, advance the welfare of the nation and deal kindly and truly with all Israel'.

In the orthodox synagogue this is the only prayer to be recited in English as well as in Hebrew and affords both a momentary relief to the visitor who knows no Hebrew and also an assurance, if that were needed (as all too often in their long and isolated history it has been), that there is nothing but loyalty on the part of the Jews to the country in which they live and of which, either by birth or adoption, the vast majority are citizens.

This brief and, from the visitor's point of view, refreshing linguistic oasis is normally followed by a sermon, also in English. For the visitor to the synagogue it has an interest all its own, both for the insights it reveals and the methods of study it reflects. As an institution it dates back well into pre-Christian times.

Much has been written about preaching by many experts, Christian no less than Jewish. Few, if any, have summed up its purpose better than a former British Chief Rabbi, Dr Hermann Adler, who wrote:

> The supreme object of preaching must ever be to lead souls unto God; to wean men and women from the pursuit of low and earthly aims to all that is good, pure and true; to build up within them the grace of patience, the power of self-discipline and the instinct of loving helpfulness, the spirit of sacrifice and of service. The preacher must feel deep sympathy with every single individual whom he addresses, regarding every upturned face, and none the less the faces turned away from him, as the countenance of never-dying souls whom he has to help on their earthly pilgrimage.

Finally there comes a brief additional (*mussaf*) service which begins with a further repetition of the *amidah*, the singing of a hymn: 'There is none like our God', and one of the greatest of all prayers in any liturgy whether Jewish, Christian or Muslim. It was indeed a great Islamic teacher in the seventeenth century who is reported to have said of it: 'Truly, this prayer is sufficient for all purposes: there is no need of any other'. It is the prayer with which every official service ends, whether it be on the Sabbath, a weekday or a festival. It is a prayer of which it may be said, as it was of the *Shema*, that it is understood and discerned, marked, learned, taught, heeded and carried out in love:

It is our duty to praise the Lord of all things,
to ascribe greatness to him who formed the world in the beginning,
Since he hath not made us like the nations of other lands,
And hath not placed us like other families of the earth,
Since he hath not assigned to us a portion as unto them,
Nor a lot as unto all their multitude.

For we bend the knee and offer worship and thanks
Before the supreme King of kings, the Holy One, blessed be he,
Who stretched forth the heavens
And laid the foundations of the earth,
The seat of whose glory is in the heavens above,
And the abode of whose might is in the loftiest heights.

He is our God; there is none else;
In truth he is our King; there is none besides him;
As it is written in the Law,
And thou shalt know this day, and lay it to thine heart,
That the Lord is God
In heaven above and upon the earth beneath:
There is none else.

We therefore hope in thee, O Lord our God,
That we may speedily behold the glory of thy might,
When thou wilt remove the abominations from the earth,
And the idols will be utterly cut off,
When the world will be perfected
Under the kingdom of the Almighty,
And all the children of flesh will call upon thy name,
When thou wilt turn upon thyself all the wicked of the earth.

Let all the inhabitants of the world perceive and know
That unto thee every knee must bow, every tongue must swear,
Before thee, O Lord our God let them bow and fall;
And unto thy glorious name let them give honour;
Let them all accept the yoke of thy kingdom,
And do thou reign over them speedily,
And for ever and ever.

For the Kingdom is thine,
And to all eternity thou wilt reign in glory;
As it is written in thy Law,
The Lord shall reign for ever and ever.
And it is said,
And the Lord shall be King over all the earth:
In that day shall the Lord be One, and his name One.

Officially the service is ended. There is however one further act of loving remembrance shared by the whole congregation with those of its members who are either recently bereaved or who are commemorating the anniversary of a loved one's death. At this point the mourners move into the aisle of the synagogue and recite what is known as the mourner's *kaddish*.

The word *kaddish* is clearly linked with the word *kiddush* which we met earlier. It means 'sanctification' and has to do with the sanctification of the name of God ('hallowed be thy name'). The prayer itself has in fact already been recited several times earlier in the Service where it has nothing whatever to do with mourning, nor indeed has it in this particular context. It is simply an ascription of praise and an affirmation of faith. The use of it by the mourners is an indication of the measure of their faith in God, of their acceptance of his will, even in the face of the loss of their loved ones, and of their confidence in the ultimate establishment of his Kingdom and the gift of his peace.

Mourner: 'Magnified and sanctified be his great Name in the world which he hath created according to his will. May he establish his kingdom during your life and during your days, and during the life of all the house of Israel, even speedily and at a near time and say ye, Amen.'

Congregation and Mourner: 'Let his great Name be blessed for ever and to all eternity.'

Mourner: 'Blessed, praised and glorified, exalted, extolled and honoured, magnified and lauded be the Name of the Holy One, blessed be he; though he be high above all the blessing and hymns, praises and consolations, which are uttered in the world; and say ye, Amen.'

Congregation: 'Amen'.

Mourner: 'He who maketh peace in high places, may he make peace for us and for all Israel, and say ye, Amen.'

Then, as a final leave-taking, the hymn: *Adon Olam* is sung. It is one of the most popular and at the same time most profound of all the hymns of the synagogue and the home, expressing complete trust in God, not only in the evening and the morning of every day, but in life, and death and that which lies beyond: a veritable gate of heaven.

A Date with a Calendar

Calendars are as fascinating as they are useful especially when they come in the form of a diary. That can be in any one of a host of different varieties. Indeed almost every kind of educational institution, social or sports organisation appears to have its own. So do a wide range of religious bodies and associations.

This is where we come in. There is of course a Christian calendar: a way of reckoning the year which begins with Advent on the first Sunday of December and continues through Christmas, Epiphany, Lent, Passiontide, Easter, Ascension, Pentecost and Trinity to a whole series of Sundays after Trinity or, as it is now becoming more fashionable to reckon, after Pentecost.

At this point we may detect a direct link with the Jewish religious Calendar which according to the *Mishnah*, the first great compilation of Rabbinic teaching made about the year 200 A.D. of the current era boasts four New Year days. The first is for reckoning the years of a king's reign and the dates of festivals. There is a New Year for the tithing of cattle. A third is for reckoning the years of release and jubilee years and also for planting trees and vegetables (a wonderful mixture that!). Finally there is a New Year for fruit trees. Of these the most important is the first, particularly because it is concerned with the dating of the major religious festivals of which Pentecost is one. It is indeed the one which provides the most obvious link with the Christian year, at least in the English version of the calendar. The French calendar in fact provides an additional link. There what we call the Easter Festival is referred to as *Paques*. This is directly derived from the Hebrew word for Passover: *Pesach*. The events which the Christian celebrates at Easter were of course coincidental with the Jewish festival of Passover in the year in which Jesus was crucified. This should mean that if all other things were equal Passover and Easter and indeed the Christian and Jewish festivals of Pentecost ought always to coincide. But, of course, things are not equal and the coincidence is only intermittent.

The reason for this is that while Jews and Christians agree with the rest of the human family in their reckoning of time in minutes, hours and days and even days in the week, they differ, religiously at any rate, in their reckoning of the number of days in the month. In Biblical times great importance was attached to the phases of the moon. The appearance of the new moon was observed as a festival and the length of a month determined by the number of days which elapsed between one new moon and the next. This is a period of approximately twenty-nine-and-a-half days. But since fractions in the reckoning of days make for difficulty in determining the number of days in the month the makers of the calendar settled for an alternating pattern of twenty-nine and thirty days each.

The situation was still further complicated, however, by the fact that the earth in its orbit round the sun takes just a fraction over 365 days. In so doing it determines the regularity and the sequence of the seasons, a sequence which neither Jew, Christian, nor anyone else can afford to ignore. This too creates its problems, even for the non-Jew, for there is no simple way of dividing 365 into equal parts.

The general solution with which we are all familiar has been to divide the year into twelve months of unequal length: seven of thirty-one days, four of thirty and one of twenty-eight. Even this, however, does not provide the perfect answer, since the solar year comprises 365 days plus a fraction of a day. This difficulty has been overcome by inserting an additional day into the twenty-eight-day month every fourth, or leap, year.

For the Jews, however, the problem was more difficult. Twelve months of alternating twenty-nine and thirty days each produce only 354 days, eleven short of the solar year of 365. This deficiency was made good by adding not an odd day or days here and there, but an additional month at regular intervals. Thus seven times in every nineteen years the Jewish religious calendar contains thirteen, not twelve, months.

To many people nowadays this may seem a lot of fuss about very little. There have been campaigns for the introduction of calendar reforms designed to iron out even the seemingly minor variations in the general calendar. Some have also proposed that the dates of such religious festivals as Easter should be so fixed that they would always fall on the same day in any year.

While for all practical purposes Jews as well as Christians have long since settled for the normal January 1st to December 31st calendar, both have shown the greatest reluctance to abandon the liturgical tradition of their respective religious years. This is because certain of the major religious festivals are particularly associated with historical events which can be precisely dated.

For example Passover and Pentecost both in the Jewish and Christian traditions are directly associated with great divine events of deliverance and rebirth: in the case of the Jews with their deliverance from the bondage of Egypt, and fifty days later at Mount Sinai with the birth of a nation, and in the Christian tradition with the deliverance of mankind from the bondage of evil and the birth of the Church as the community of the redeemed.

According to the Biblical story the Passover or the Exodus from Egypt took place on the 15th day of the Jewish month of Nisan, which, whether in a leap year or not, always falls in the March/April period. And since the first day of the month always coincided with the new moon it is obvious that the exodus from Egypt would have occurred on the night of the full moon.

To the sophisticated twentieth-century reader, interested only in naturalistic or scientific explanations it may seem of little consequence whether in fact the Exodus happened in Nisan or any other month, though the association of the event with the night of a full moon may give some point to a certain strategic interpretation. For those who still cling to the belief that 'there are more things in heaven and earth than are dreamed of' in most people's philosophies, or indeed in scientific text books, there is something to be said for the preservation of a tradition which traces the hand of God in the historical event, even if it means observing two calendars.

The same is true for the Christians, and explains the widespread resistance to the idea of a fixed Easter which at first sight has much to commend it. Particularly is this the case when one turns to the tables in the Anglican Book of Common Prayer for reckoning the date of Easter. We know from the Gospel records, however, that the death of Jesus occurred in a year in which the first day of the Feast of the Passover occurred on a Friday. From this it followed that the resurrection which is claimed to have taken place on 'the third day' must have happened on the following Sunday.

But here a difficulty arises. While it is of little consequence to the Jew on which day of the week the anniversary of the Passover (the 15th day of Nisan) occurs, it is of very great importance for the Christian that Easter be celebrated on a Sunday, the 'first day of the week' according to Biblical reckoning. The dating of Easter Sunday is, therefore, determined by the first full moon which occurs upon or next after March 21st, which is the day of the Spring equinox.

There is one other interesting and important difference between the Jewish and Christian methods of reckoning time. For the Christian historic time is determined by whether an event occurred B.C. (before Christ) or A.D. (*anno domini*, or in the year of the Lord). For Jews for whom the coming of Christ is not the crux of the historical process this terminology is clearly unacceptable. They therefore speak of events as occurring B.C.E. (before the common era) or C.E. (within the common era).

Liturgically, however, they follow a system all, or nearly all, their own. The standard reference book of the Anglo-Jewish community, The Jewish Year Book, carries on the cover of the current issue two dates: 1975 and 5735/6. The first is obvious. But why the second? Lovers of the King James (Authorised) version of the English Bible may remember that at the head of the column of marginal references for the first chapter of Genesis there occurs the figure 4004 B.C. This, according to the reckoning of Archbishop Ussher, a seventeenth-century divine, was the date of the creation of the world. Add to this the 1975 'years of our Lord', and we arrive at the figure 5979 which approximates recognisably to, but is not identical with, the date on the Jewish Year Book 5735/6. The reason for the difference lies simply in the variant reckoning of the genealogies of the Hebrew Bible as between the Rabbis and the learned Archbishop. The Jewish liturgical calendar therefore dates ostensibly from the creation of the world.

But surely no one takes this seriously today. In one sense, no. There can be few if any today, whether Jews or Christians, who would seriously maintain that the world was created less than six thousand years ago. As long ago as the twelfth century (C.E. or A.D.) Moses Maimonides wrote: 'The account given in the Scripture of the Creation is not, as is generally believed, intended to be in all its parts literal'. Much has happened since then, and scientists have made it clear beyond all peradventure that whatever views we

may hold about the origin of this material universe, we continue to exist in a space/time dimension which beggars all imagining.

Yet there is a sense in which the double dating of the Jewish Year Book stands for something of quite fundamental importance. When the astronomers, the physicists, the geologists, the mathematicians and a host of others have told us all they know their answers serve only to raise further questions rather than to solve our fundamental problem. Man must begin somewhere in his attempt to find a place for himself and for the whole story of the human family in this vast empyrean of universes. And where better can he begin than with the sublimely simple affirmation with which the Hebrew Bible opens: 'In the beginning, when the earth was without form and void (all *tohu va bohu* as the Hebrew so vividly has it), God said: "Let there be light", and there was light'.

A calendar then may be fascinating. It is certainly useful. But for those who have eyes to see, it can also be a veritable means of grace.

Harvests and History

History, then, for the Jew is much more than a mere chronicle of events. Ideally at least it is the evidence to be adduced in support of his basic faith that God is at work in the happenings of past and present alike. The belief that:

> There's a divinity that shapes our ends,
> Rough-hew them how we will

was endemic in Jewish life and thought long before Shakespeare put these much quoted lines into the mouth of Hamlet. What others might regard as important historic anniversaries are in the Jewish calendar essentially religious festivals.

Long ante-dating his interest in history, however, was the awareness he shared with his fellow-men of their common dependence upon the miracle and the mystery of the harvest. The earliest festivals therefore in the Jewish as in so many other religious calendars were harvest festivals. And since the Israelites had settled on the fringe of the fertile crescent they had not one, but three harvests to celebrate each year. The first was the barley harvest which ripened just about the middle of the month of Nisan. This was followed some two months later by the gathering of the first fruits: the grapes, figs, pomegranates, olives and dates, which thrive in those parts. At this season also the wheat was harvested. Finally, in the early autumn came the Feast of the Ingathering. The equivalent of the 'Harvest Home'.

Upon these early celebrations of the harvest there was later imposed a pattern of three major historical festivals: Passover, Pentecost and Tabernacles in the celebration of which traces of the original agricultural association are still to be found. Thus for example on the second day of Passover (Nisan 16th) it is customary to begin counting the *omer* which is here interpreted as the first sheaf from the barley harvest which was taken to the Temple and ceremoniously 'waved before the Lord' on the second day of the Passover festival.

From this first offering forty-nine days were counted until on the fiftieth, the day of Pentecost, the Festival of the First Fruits was celebrated (Deuteronomy 26:1-11). Here we can see clearly how the agricultural and the historical significance of the festivals came to be so closely interrelated. When the worshipper had offered to the priest in the Temple a basket containing the first fruits of his land he was required solemnly to recite before the Lord his God: 'My father was a homeless Aramaean who went down to Egypt with a small company and lived there until they became a great, powerful, and numerous nation. But the Egyptians ill-treated us, humiliated us and imposed cruel slavery upon us. Then we cried to the Lord the God of our fathers for help, and he listened to us and saw our humiliation, our hardship and distress; and so the Lord brought us out of Egypt with a strong hand and outstretched arm, with terrifying deeds, and with signs and portents. He brought us to this place and gave us his land, a land flowing with milk and honey. And now I have brought the first fruits of the soil which thou, O Lord, has given to me'. He then left the basket before the altar and bowed down in worship before the Lord his God. This tradition has survived until the present time only in the decoration of the synagogue at Pentecost with flowers and fruit.

The agricultural associations of the third of the three major festivals, Tabernacles, are deep-rooted, clear and very domestic. Commencing on the 15th day of the seventh month of the liturgical year (*Tishri*) the festival coincides, like Passover, with a full moon; this time the harvest moon. Wherever it is practically possible the family erect some form of temporary shelter (a tabernacle or booth) either in the garden or on some balcony or verandah, which they decorate with fruit and foliage and in which they take at least some meals during the eight days of the festival. In addition there will almost certainly be a communal tabernacle or *succah* in the synagogue.

Like all harvest festivals, Tabernacles was a season of great rejoicing. Even in Biblical times there were great illuminations in the Temple in Jerusalem. 'There was not a courtyard in Jerusalem that did not reflect its light' declared the Rabbis. 'Countless Levites played on harps, lyres, cymbals and trumpets and instruments of music, on the fifteen steps leading down from the courts of the Israelites to the court of the women, corresponding to the fifteen Songs of

Ascent in the Psalms [120 to 134]. He that has never seen the joy of this festival' they said, 'has never in his life seen joy'.

Just as they thought of the harvest as the fulfilment of a divine promise built into the very structure of the natural order that 'while the earth remaineth, seed time and harvest, and cold and heat, and summer and winter, and day and night, shall not cease', so they came to think of God's power, his justice and his providential care as being evident in the processes of history. Passover, Pentecost and Tabernacles have survived to this day as vivid reminders of the fact that he is not an absentee God, but one who having created, also sustains his people (and not his 'chosen' people only) fulfilling his own purpose in and through the totality of their historical experience.

Passover, the first and most popular of the three is essentially a festival of liberation, of new beginnings, celebrating as it does the deliverance of the Children of Israel from the bondage of Egypt. It is a festival in which it is becoming almost customary to invite some non-Jewish friends to participate. Basically, of course, it is a family occasion and every member of the family who can will be present for what in Hebrew is known as the *seder*. The word itself means simply 'order' and is intended to convey, what is in fact the case, that on this of all nights everything is done 'decently and in order'. From first to last everything follows an order, or pattern as lovely as it is beloved. It is centred around the narration, the *Haggadah* of the story of how the Lord brought his people out of the bondage of Egypt and set them on the way to the Promised Land.

The text of this 'narration' is set out in the service book, or *Haggadah*, with which every guest is provided. In earlier days, before the development of printing, the *Haggadah* was a very precious volume. Written by hand, in Hebrew of course, it was frequently decorated and illuminated in very much the style of the Roman missal. Today it is printed in a wide range of styles from the very simple to the highly ornate, with the text almost invariably in Hebrew and in the vernacular.

The Passover is also known as the Feast of Unleavened Bread, to commemorate the fact that on the night they left Egypt everything had to be done with the utmost despatch and there was not time to wait for the leavening of the dough with which they made their bread. The *matzah* or unleavened bread is popularly known as the 'bread of affliction'. It is eaten, not only on the first night but throughout the whole of the eight days of the festival. Nor do Jews eat any kind of food containing leaven or any other fermenting agent.

The table has as its centre-piece a special plate or dish on which are arranged a piece of roasted shank bone of lamb, a roasted egg, some bitter herbs (horse-radish, for example), a bowl of salt-water, and a paste made of grated apple, ground nuts and cinnamon known as *haroseth*, a word of unknown origin but thought by some to derive from a word meaning 'clay'.

As we might expect, every ingredient of this strange '*hors d'oeuvre*' has its symbolic part to play. Thus the *haroseth*, though a real delicacy, is intended to recall the clay from which the Israelites were compelled to make bricks without straw (Exodus 5:6); the bitter herbs the bitterness of a people's suffering; and the roasted shank bone the passover lamb. The meaning of the roasted egg, in which it is difficult not to see some analogy with the easter egg, is more problematic. While some have interpreted it as a symbol of sorrow and sacrifice, others see in it the promise of a new life.

And so the stage is set for the re-enactment of one of the oldest and most fascinating of all domestic rituals. It opens with the ceremonial act of sanctification, the blessing of the wine and the bread, albeit unleavened bread on this occasion, and the *kiddush* with which all festival meals begin. Then, after the brief 'grace before meat' one of the younger members of the family asks the senior member, the father or the grandfather, the time-honoured question: 'Why is this night different from all other nights?'.

Why indeed? 'For', the questioner continues, 'on all other nights we can eat bread or *matzah* (unleavened bread): why, tonight, only *matzah*? On all other nights, we can eat any kind of herbs: why, tonight, bitter herbs? On all other nights, we don't dip the herbs we eat into anything: why, tonight, do we dip them twice (first into salt-water and then into *haroseth*)? On all other nights, we can eat either sitting up straight or reclining: why, tonight, do we all recline?'

The answer is as simple as, at first sight, the question seems involved. 'We were slaves to Pharaoh in Egypt', it begins, and continues with the reminder that 'God brought us out from there "with a strong hand and an outstretched arm".' This is the heart of the matter. All the rest is commentary. Fascinating, exciting, stimulating, but commentary nonetheless. In true rabbinic style this includes a discussion of when and for how long the story should be told. This is followed by a review of the history of the Children of Israel from the call of Abraham to their arrival in Egypt, their sufferings under 'the Pharaoh who knew not Joseph'. It recounts the story of the ten plagues, the prelude to their escape. In all this there is no reference to the part played by Moses. The emphasis is always upon the Lord who delivered them with his 'strong hand and outstretched arm'. Then, as if unable to contain themselves any longer, the whole company seated around the table bursts into a song of praise and rejoicing:

> What abundant favours has the Almighty bestowed upon us.
>
> If he had only brought us out of Egypt and not inflicted judgment upon the Egyptians: *dayenu* [it would have sufficed].
>
> If he had only inflicted judgment upon the Egyptians and not upon their gods: it would have sufficed ...

and so on, *dayenu, dayenu, dayenu* until the whole saga of deliverance is recapitulated in a paean of praise which begins:

> How much then are we indebted for the manifold blessings conferred upon us by the Almighty.

and ends with the reflection that:

> He supplied us with everything in the wilderness for forty years: gave us manna to eat: gave us the Sabbath: led us to Mount Sinai: gave us his law: led us into the land of Israel: and built the holy Temple for us to make atonement for all our sins.

And all this is sung, as are so many of the psalms and songs of the *Haggadah*, to a rollicking melody which can only serve to heighten the sense of rejoicing and which has an uncanny way of living in the memory from one Passover celebration to the next, as characteristic and as unforgettable as many of the carols Christians associate with Christmas.

But the heart of the matter lies in the opening affirmation. It does not say our fathers, or our ancestors 'were slaves to Pharaoh in Egypt'. Still less does it refer to some vague 'they'. The *Haggadah* begins with precise and immediate relevance: 'We were slaves'. Involvement is total. In Jewish history past and present merge mysteriously into one timeless self-identification with a people for whom 'Egypt' has all too often been the here and now, and 'Pharaoh' any one of a tragic succession of tyrants culminating in the horrors of the Nazi holocaust. 'In every generation', it is said, 'a Jew should see himself as if he had personally come out of Egypt.' And in every generation he should remember that his deliverance was achieved, not by his own power or might, but by 'the strong hand and outstretched arm' of the Lord his God.

This vivid evocation of the past, with its story-telling, its symbolic *hors d'oeuvre* and its cheerful songs, is followed by the meal proper: a leisurely interlude, enlivened by the eagerly welcomed opportunity for the exchange of family news, a commodity never in short supply in any Jewish family.

But the end is not yet. After the meal comes grace which on *seder* night is augmented by several features special to the occasion. There comes a solemn moment, for example, when the outside door of the house is opened to remind the celebrants, it is said by some, how near at hand is the unfriendly world at the hands of which they have suffered so much so often.

The solemnity of the moment is heightened by the recitation of three verses from the Psalms (79:6-7 and 69:25) and one from Lamentations (3:66) invoking the wrath of God upon 'the heathen that have not known thee'. For the majority of Jews today this is an embarrassing moment, especially if there are non-Jewish guests present, but for both it becomes understandable, at least when taken in the light of a history which all too often has inspired even if it has not justified such feelings.

The mood quickly changes however with the performance of the last of the symbolic acts of the evening, the pouring out of a cup of wine for Elijah the prophet whose return, according to the prophet Malachi, is to herald the dawn of the messianic age. Then comes the *Hallel*, the great hymn of praise comprising Psalms 115 to 118 and concluding with Psalm 136, which encompasses the whole story of God's providential care from the creation of the world, through the deliverance from Egypt to the settlement in the Promised Land, the whole Psalm being punctuated by the constantly reiterated refrain: 'for his mercy endureth for ever'.

This was almost certainly 'the hymn' mentioned in Saint Mark (14:26) after the singing of which Jesus and his disciples went out from the last supper, which in all probability was itself the passover meal, to the Mount of Olives.

The spirit of unbounded gratitude is nowhere better expressed in the Jewish or any other liturgy than in a paragraph from the prayer which follows the singing of the *Hallel*:

> Though our mouths were full of song as the sea,
> And our tongues of exultation as the multitude of its waters
> And our lips with praises as the expanses of the firmament;
> Though our eyes were radiant like the sun and the moon,
> And our hands were spread forth like the eagles of heaven
> And our feet were swift as hinds,
> We should yet be unable to thank thee
> O Lord our God and God of our fathers
> Even for one in a thousand
> Of the many thousands of thousands
> And myriad of myriads of kindnesses
> That thou hast wrought upon our fathers and upon us.

And so the final petition that the *seder*, the Passover service, thus completed 'in accordance with all its ordinances and statutes' will prove acceptable to God and to the final triumphant expression of an unquenchable hope: 'Next year in Jerusalem'.

The rest is pure relaxation. Reluctant to break up the party, the family, including the children who look forward to this as perhaps the most exciting part of the evening, stay together round the table to sing a number of traditional songs including two, which in their general pattern, will be very familiar to any non-Jewish visitor: 'Who know One?' and 'One only kid'.

The first is closely parallel to the well-known English folk-song: 'Green grow the rushes, O!'. Both are derivative, probably of medieval origin. Both have religious and biblical associations, each starting from an affirmation about the unity of God: 'One is one and all alone and evermore shall be so'. 'Green grow the rushes' has twelve verses; 'Who know one', thirteen: perhaps because the letters which make up the word 'One' in Hebrew, in their numerical connotation (for Hebrew had no separate numerical system) together add up to thirteen. Whatever the explanation, however, the thirteenth verse of the Hebrew song, which recapitulates also the preceding twelve, is as follows:

> Who knows Thirteen? Thirteen I know!
> Thirteen are the attributes of God:
> Twelve are the Tribes:
> Eleven are the Stars:
> Ten are the Commandments:
> Nine are the months of Carrying:
> Eight are the days of the Covenant:
> Seven are the days of the Week:
> Six are the Orders of the Mishnah:
> Five are the Books of the Law:
> Four are the Mothers:
> Three are the Fathers:
> Two are the Tables of Covenant:
> One is our God in Heaven and on Earth.

The second follows very much the pattern of 'The House that Jack Built', beginning with:

> One only kid
> That father bought for two zuzim
>
> Then came a cat
> And ate the kid

and so on until ...

> Then came the Holy One,
>   Blessed be he
> And smote the Angel of Death
> That slew the slaughterer
> That slaughtered the ox
> That drank the water
> That quenched the fire
> That burned the stick
> That beat the dog
> That bit the cat
> That ate the kid
> That father bought for two zuzim
> One only kid, One only kid.

And the meaning of this piece of seeming nonsense? As with so many other things in Jewish life it is given a symbolic interpretation in which the kid is taken as referring to Israel, which was acquired as a perpetual possession by his heavenly Father with the two tables of the Law. What follows is a bird's-eye-view of Jewish history in which the cat is said to represent Assyria, the dog Babylon and the stick Persia. Greece which engulfed Persia is represented by the water. Rome is represented by the ox which in turn overcame Greece; the slaughterer, the Moslems and the angel of death the European nations who eventually overcame the Moslems, until finally 'the Holy One, blessed be He' arrived to re-establish the principles of justice on earth and to rescue his people from the hands of their successive oppressors.

And finally, as if all this were not enough, it is customary in some households to wind up the whole evening by reading the Song of Songs which, in any event, is read on the Sabbath which falls within the octave of the festival. Its relevance is obvious. It is essentially a spring song:

> For lo the winter is past,
> The rain is over and gone,
> The flowers appear on the earth,
> The time of the singing of the birds has come
> And the voice of the turtle-dove
> is heard in our land.

Once the rabbis had decided that this superb collection of love poems was to be interpreted in terms of the relation between God and his people its association with Passover was thought of in terms of God's deliverance of his beloved Israel and their eventual marriage in the Sinaitic covenant.

To have lingered so long over Passover is to have followed a good Jewish tradition. There is always a marked reluctance to break up the *Seder* night party which has undisputed pride of place among the great historic festivals. From Passover everything else follows, and first, of course, Pentecost or the Feast of Weeks (*Shavuoth*).

The weeks are the seven mentioned in Leviticus (23: 15) and are counted from the second day of Passover. Indeed the two festivals are so closely linked that Pentecost was first called *Atzereth*, which means 'conclusion', implying that it was simply the completion of the Passover Festival. Moreover the festival has yet another name: *zeman matan toratenu*, 'the season of the giving of the Law'. It is a great thing to be liberated. It is even more important to understand why and to what end. One of our major contemporary problems rises from the fact that so many liberation movements lack any clear idea of how to achieve the new and free society, the longing for which inspired their struggle to escape from the bondage of the old. They have not yet reached the Sinaitic stage.

This feeling of continuity was beautifully expressed by Moses Maimonides who wrote: 'We count the days that pass since the preceding Festival, just as one who expects his most intimate friend on a certain day, counts the days and even the hours. This is the reason why we count the days that pass since the offering of the *omer*, between the anniversary of our departure from Egypt and the anniversary of the Law-giving, for this was the aim and object of the exodus from Egypt.'

Christians too would do well to remember that the Pentecost we celebrate as the festival of the giving of

the Holy Spirit was known to, and had already been celebrated during his lifetime by, Jesus, as the festival of the giving of the Law. It is even more important to realise that there is no dichotomy between these two. Separated from Sinai the experience in the upper room may easily prove as destructive as some contemporary liberation movements in the political sphere.

In Jewish circles the festival still retains something of the character of a harvest festival. Synagogues are decorated with flowers and foliage, and the home enriched with dairy foods, especially milk and honey, the all-time reminders of the Promised Land and of the Law which according to the Psalmist was 'sweeter than honey and the honeycomb' (Psalm 19:10). Cheesecake is another delicacy specially associated with Pentecost.

In the synagogue the principal focus of interest is upon the Law. There was a time when the more devout members of the congregation used to spend the whole of the first night of the festival in study. The special readings for the morning service on the first day of the festival tell how the Law was given on Mount Sinai and also what sacrifices were offered in the Temple on festival occasions (Exodus 19:20; Numbers 28). On the second day the reading which is associated also with Passover and Tabernacles, sets out the details for celebrating all three festivals (Deuteronomy 14:16).

Reference to the 'second' day calls for some explanation. Why should the 'fiftieth day' be celebrated on the fifty-first also? The answer takes us back to our

84

'date with a calendar' and opens yet another window into the meticulous devotion with which Jews have for so long ordered their religious life and observance. In ancient times when there was neither a Greenwich Observatory nor any system of telecommunications, it was not easy to ensure that everyone knew just when the new moon had appeared and a new month begun. Responsibility for spreading the news rested upon the President and members of the *Sanhedrin* (the Jewish ecclesiastical court). A chain of beacon fires, starting in Jerusalem, provided an obvious solution. This worked well enough until the Samaritans deliberately confused the method by setting off the beacons prematurely. It became necessary to resort to personal messengers, and since this clearly involved delay the doubling of the first day of certain major festivals was instituted.

For the historian the practice is both interesting and understandable. The current observance, however, appears to many within and outside the Jewish community to be both anachronistic and unnecessarily complicated, interfering as it frequently appears to do with school discipline and business efficiency. In Israel, of course, it was never observed and Liberal and Reform Jews have abandoned the 'second day'.

Apart from a natural reluctance to abandon a tradition so long established the orthodox Jew, however, faces two major practical problems. First, this is only one of many customs which have long outlived their practical purpose. If one should go, then why not all the rest? The second, and even more difficult, is the problem of how to effect the change, however desirable it may appear to many to be. The fact is that there does not exist in Jewry today any central religious authority competent to pronounce on such matters in a way that could hope to command general acceptance. This is not specially a Jewish problem. In principle it is shared in varying degree by other religious communities. Fellow feeling should indeed make us understanding as well as kind. Alas that we still have so far to travel in this direction.

Two other points are of general interest. First, the story of Ruth is prescribed reading for Pentecost. The reason is obvious. It is one of the loveliest harvest stories of all time. But there is more to it than that. As a story of human love, devotion and loyalty it is of unsurpassable beauty. It has its universal implications too. Its heroine, Ruth, was a Moabitess, a daughter of a people reckoned among Israel's most bitter enemies. Yet she, of all people, was destined to become the great-grandmother of King David and an ancestress of the Messiah whose coming is still awaited 'with perfect faith'.

And finally there is a wonderful hymn which has for some hundreds of years been closely identified with Pentecost. It is attributed to a certain Rabbi Meir who lived during the second half of the eleventh century and whose wife and son were martyred during the first Crusade in 1096. The hymn is written in Aramaic and has come to be known by its opening word: *akdamuth*. Its theme is the glory of God, the wonder of the *Torah* and Israel's loyalty to it. It is sung in the synagogue on the first day of the festival, just before the reading of the *Torah*. The opening verse, by which it has become widely known, splendidly expresses the spirit of the Festival as a whole:

Could we with ink the ocean fill,
Were every blade of grass a quill,
Were the whole world of prachment made,
And every man a scribe by trade,
   To write the love
   Of God above
Would drain that ocean dry;
   Nor would the scroll
   Contain the whole,
Though stretched from sky to sky.

Tabernacles (*Succoth*), the third of the three major festivals of history, falls in the late summer or early autumn. Known also as 'the season of our joy' (*zeman simchatenu*), it was as we have already seen primarily a harvest festival. It is possible that the booths, from which it takes its name, were the temporary structures which they used to construct in the vineyards and olive groves during the harvest period. In Leviticus (23:42), however, we find the more familiar interpretation. There the Israelites were told to 'dwell in booths seven days ... that your generations may know that I made the children of Israel to dwell in booths, when I brought them out of the land of Egypt'.

Today, when literal obedience to this command is virtually ruled out by the conditions of modern life, the majority of Jews living in urban centres take advantage of a communal *succah* or booth that is built into a synagogue. There services, social events take place, and even the occasional meal can be served in token fulfilment of the command to 'dwell in booths'. It is an essential feature of the *succah* that the roof should not be completely enclosed so that the sky is always visible.

Among the customs specially associated with the festival is that every worshipper in the synagogue carries a *lulav* or spray of foliage. This is in fulfilment of the command in Leviticus (23:40): 'On the first day you shall take the fruit of citrus trees, palm fronds and leafy branches, and willows from the riverside and you shall rejoice before the Lord your God for seven days'.

As so often happens, this simple act lent itself to all kinds of symbolic interpretations. Thus, for example, the citron, palm, myrtle and willow, were interpreted by the Rabbis as symbolising four types of men. Thus the citron, which has both taste and fragrance, represents those with learning and good deeds. The palm, with taste but no fragrance, those who have learning but no good deeds. Those with good deeds but no learning are symbolised by the myrtle, which has fragrance but not taste, while the willow, with neither taste nor fragrance, represents those with neither learning nor good deeds. Even these last, the Rabbis taught, are bound up with the others since, in the eyes of the Holy One, they will all atone for one another. And in that hour the Lord is glorified.

The book specially selected to be read during the festival is Ecclesiastes, which seems at first sight a strange choice for the 'season of our joy'. Indeed there was a time when its suitability for inclusion in the Bible at all was hotly disputed. In the end wisdom prevailed and both the Bible and this particular festival are the richer for it. For its author was a man who recognised that life is very much a matter of contrasts, that its polarities are to be creatively absorbed rather than negatively resisted. For a man in the midst of prosperity to succumb to the temptation of supposing that he is self-sufficient would be the height of folly and the almost certain prelude to disaster. His true joy lies, not in the measure of his own achievements, but in the acknowledgment of his dependence upon the love and the goodness of God.

The festival is immediately followed by the most joyous day in the whole year: the rejoicing of the Law (*simchat torah*). On this day the annual cycle of the weekly portions of the Law is completed with the reading of the last two chapters of Deuteronomy. On this same day the cycle is renewed in returning to the opening of Genesis.

When the reading is completed all the Scrolls are taken from the ark to be carried in triumphal procession seven times round the synagogue by the 'bridegrooms of the Law', members of the congregation whose signal honour it is to have been chosen for just this purpose. This procession is more of a dance than a stately progress, recalling the day on which in sheer delight at its recovery from the hands of the Philistines David danced before the ark of the Lord.

Again the spirit of the whole festival is delightfully reflected in the following verses which are sung almost at the end of the day:

> The Angels came a-mustering
>   A-mustering, a-mustering,
> The Angels came a-mustering
>   Around the sapphire throne.
>
> A-questioning of one another,
>   Of one another, of one another,
> A-questioning each one his brother
>   Around the sapphire throne.
>
> Pray who is he, and where is he,
>   And where is he, and where is he,
> Whose shining casts—so fair is he—
>   A shadow on the throne?

Pray, who has up to heaven come,
To heaven come, to heaven come,
Through all the circles seven come,
To fetch the Torah down?

'Tis Moses up to heaven come,
To heaven come, to heaven come,
Through all the circles seven come,
To fetch the Torah down.

So the festival which begins by recalling under the image of the tabernacle the transitoriness of human life ends in the joyful affirmation of confidence in the things that are eternal.

There are two other historical festivals in the calendar.

The first, *Purim*, occurs in the spring. Its name, a Persian word, is connected with the casting of lots. The events commemorated are those recorded in the story of Esther, another of the books which found its way into the Bible only after the gravest doubts. Its inspiration was seriously questioned. There is no mention of God nor any reference to prayers either of petition or thanksgiving, while the militant anti-gentile character of its concluding chapters was viewed with anxiety by the rabbis who feared they might prove counter-productive in arousing hatred among others.

But it is a good story: one of the best of its kind. It tells of the overthrow of tyrants who, from Pharaoh to Hitler have threatened to destroy the Jewish minorities under their domination. One of the features of the celebration is the reading of the story (the whole of the book of Esther) in the synagogue in very much of a carnival atmosphere. The 'audience participation' is vociferous when, to the accompaniment of rattles and the stamping of feet every reference to Haman, the arch-villain, is booed, while every mention of Mordechai and Esther is greeted with cheers. It is also very much a children's occasion when the story is told dramatically in mime or play.

But just because such enthusiasm can so easily stir up feelings of hatred the rabbis have been careful to emphasise that the regulations which govern the celebration of *Purim* 'are not intended to commemorate revenge, vindictiveness and the downfall of our enemies, but to keep ever-green in our minds the hope of the ultimate triumph of that which is just'. Their aim is to foster the understandable belief that 'the Eternal One of Israel does not falsify or disappoint' (I Samuel 15:29).

The second of the minor historical festivals, *Chanukah* (dedication) commemorates an event recorded, not in the Bible itself, but in the Apocrypha. There, in the first book of Maccabees (1:41-64) we read how the Temple in Jerusalem was defiled on the 25th day of the month *Kislev*, in the year 168 B.C.E. when, at the command of the Greek conqueror Antiochus, idolatrous sacrifices were offered on the altar.

Three years later to the day, following upon the successful revolt of Judas Maccabeus and his four brothers, the Temple was re-dedicated and the *menorah* re-kindled. At this point fact and legend become strangely interwoven. One of the most popular of the legends tells how although there was only sufficient oil to keep the seven lamps of the *menorah* alight for one day, the lights lasted miraculously for eight days until fresh supplies of holy oil were prepared.

Whatever the explanation, however, it has for centuries been the custom in home and synagogue to use an eight-branch *menorah* for *Chanukah* which is marked by the lighting of one branch on the first day, two on the second, three on the third and so on until, on the eighth day the whole lampstand is ablaze with light.

As with *Purim* the rabbis were careful to insist that *Chanukah* is more than the mere celebration of a military victory. It is a symbolic reminder 'of the miracles, the deliverances and the wonders which thou, O Lord, didst work for our fathers'. The kindling of the lights, to the accompaniment of the appropriate blessings and prayers, is followed by the singing of a much-loved hymn, *ma'oz tzur* (the mighty rock) which dates back to the thirteenth century.

The second verse to the fifth tell of the exodus from Egypt, the re-building of the Temple by Zerubbabel after the Babylonian exile, the overthrow of Haman and the victory of the Maccabees. The first sets the tone for all the rest:

> Mighty, praised beyond compare,
>   Rock of my salvation,
> Build again my House of Prayer
>   For thy habitation.
> Haste my restoration; let a ransomed nation
>   Joyful sing ·
>   To its King,
> Psalms of dedication.

The very popular tune to which it is universally sung is of German origin and has also found its way into Christian hymnody.

So for the Jew, as for the Christian, history is more than a mere chronicle of events, of triumphs and disasters and all the varied facets of a people's life. It is a record of divine self-revelation, of the unfolding, for those who have eyes to see and ears to hear, of a creative and redemptive process, the end of which is not in time, but beyond time, in the eternal victory of the forces of light over all the powers of evil.

'All ... shall come'

From the particularity of a people's history we pass to the universality of man's spiritual needs as they are reflected in three other major festivals: the Sabbath, New Year and Day of Atonement. Though celebrated in a Jewish way, and primarily with a Jewish intention their real concern is with man's universal desire for peace within himself, for reconciliation with his neighbour, and the feeling of being at one with his God.

Though the observance of the Sabbath is first enjoined in the fourth of the ten commandments the institution is linked there and elsewhere with the story of the creation which tells how, after six days of intensive activity, the Lord 'rested on the seventh day and hallowed it'. Its spirit and intention are restricted neither to time, place or people. It is always and everywhere a 'day of light and rejoicing'. It looks not merely to the past but also to the future, in time and beyond time. The end of the Sabbath is in the dawn of the Messianic age.

Something of the delight with which it is observed, both in the home and the Synagogue, we have already seen. One of the many lovely things we omitted earlier, since our attention was focused on what happens in the home on the Friday evening, is the way in which the Sabbath is welcomed into the synagogue with a hymn as a bride and a queen. This hymn was written four hundred years ago by Rabbi Solomon ha-Levi, in the little town of Safed which still stands out prominently among the hills to the north of the Sea of Galilee:

> Come my beloved, with chorus of praise
> Welcome Bride Sabbath, the Queen of the Days.

When the last verse is reached, the whole congregation turn in their places to face the entrance of the synagogue as if to greet the arrival of a real presence:

> Come in thy joyousness, Crown of thy Lord,
> Come bringing peace to the folk of the Word;
> Come where the faithful in gladsome accord,
>   Hail thee as Sabbath-bride, Queen of the Days.
> Come where the faithful are hymning thy praise,
> Come as the bride cometh, Queen of the Days.

Judaism, however, is not merely a religion for the heights. Jews more than most know what it is also to plumb the depths: the depths of suffering, whether inflicted by others or borne of the realisation that in common with their fellow-men of whatever race, creed or tongue, they have sinned and fallen short of the glory of God. Penitence, confession and prayers for forgiveness have their place in every part of the liturgy, whether in the daily service or the special occasion.

Nowhere is this more apparent than in the solemn services which mark the beginning of the New Year (*Rosh Hashana*), and ten days later, *Yom Kippur*, or the Day of Atonement. The third of the four new

year days begins on the first day of the seventh month and is now everywhere known as *the* New Year. In the first instance it had an agricultural association for it was the period of the ingathering of the harvest, to be celebrated a few days later in the Feast of Tabernacles. It was, also, the day on which Ezra the Scribe read the Book of the Law of Moses to the people who had returned to Jerusalem from the Babylonian exile (Nehemiah 8:1-8). It was a day of mixed solemnity and joy, for although, as Nehemiah records, 'the people had been weeping whilst they listened to the words of the Law' they were later told that they might refresh themselves 'with rich food and sweet drinks, and send a share to all who cannot provide for themselves, for this day is holy to our Lord'.

Some of this has survived in a festive meal on the first night of the New Year in the course of which it is customary to dip a piece of bread over which grace has been recited into honey in token of the sweet year which it is hoped will follow. A piece of apple may also be dipped into honey and a prayer recited: 'May it be Thy will O Lord our God and God of our fathers to renew unto us a good and sweet year'.

The traditional New Year greeting: 'May you be inscribed (in the book of life) for a good year' reflects the teaching of the rabbis that 'three books are opened on *Rosh Hashanah*, one for the completely righteous, one for the completely wicked, and one for the average persons. The completely righteous are immediately inscribed in the book of life and the completely wicked in the book of death. The average persons are kept in suspense from *Rosh Hashanah* to the Day of Atonement. If they deserve well they are inscribed in the book of life. If not, then in the book of death.'

Though the intellectual difficulties inherent in this concept were earnestly debated during the medieval period, the theme of the 'three' books still plays an important part in the liturgy. Moreover, whatever the feeling about the imagery, the fact is that during what are commonly referred to as 'the days of awe' from New Year to the Day of Atonement Jews are careful to settle up all outstanding debts, to fulfil any outstanding obligations and to ensure that their relationships with friends and neighbours are in good shape. A man who has not made his peace with his fellow men cannot hope to be at peace with God.

The festival is known by four names, the most common of which is, of course, the New Year. Others are the day of remembrance, the day of judgment, and the day of the blowing of trumpets.

The idea of judgment no doubt stems from the rabbinic tradition that the world itself was created in the month of *Tishri* and that therefore not Israel only but the whole world will be judged on this day. Its consequent solemnity is emphasised by the blowing of trumpets: a tradition deriving from the verse in Leviticus (23:24) which, in the older translations reads: 'In the seventh month, in the first day of the month, shall be a solemn rest unto you, a memorial proclaimed with the blast of horns, a holy convocation'. In the New English Bible the 'blast of horns' has been replaced by the neutral though linguistically permissible word 'acclamation', thus obscuring the Biblical root of a tradition still universally observed in synagogues throughout the world.

The horn (*shofar*), is the horn of a ram, reminiscent of the ram caught by its horn in the thicket at the binding of Isaac, and not of a cow or a calf, which would recall the idolatrous lapse of the Israelites at the foot of Mount Sinai. The notes played have an eerie, haunting quality, well calculated to engender the emotions they are intended to express; of weeping, groaning and wailing. Their proper enunciation is very much the task of a specialist.

'The scriptural injunction of the *shofar* for the New Year Day', wrote Moses Maimonides, 'has a profound meaning. It says: "Awake, ye sleepers, and ponder over your deeds, remember your Creator and go back to Him in penitence. Be not of those who miss realities in their pursuit of shadows and waste their years in seeking after vain things which cannot profit or deliver. Look well to your souls and consider your acts; forsake each of you his evil ways and thoughts, and return to God so that He may have mercy upon you".'

Jewish the idiom may be, but the pursuit of shadows and the seeking after vain things are in no sense peculiarly Jewish preoccupations. It may be a characteristic flight of rabbinical fantasy to claim that the world was created in the Hebrew month of *Tishri*, but the measure of the Jewish New Year, whether its celebrants recognise it or not, is of universal application. The judgment is one to which not Jews only but all the world must come. But the judgment is not the end. Ten days later comes the Day of Atonement (*Yom Kippur*) and solemn though its observance is, its climax is one of confident and joyous affirmation of faith in a God who does not let his anger rage for ever and delights in love that will not change (Micah 7:18).

The Biblical passage describing the observance of the Day of Atonement is read as the portion of the Law for the morning service on that day. It tells of the dress to be worn by the High Priest and of the sacrifices to be offered, including the strange custom of driving out a goat, a scapegoat, into the wilderness as a sin-offering. More to the point of contemporary interest is the thought of the day as a 'Sabbath of rest' on which the people were to 'afflict their souls', or mortify themselves as the New English Bible has it, and to make expiation for their sins before God. For, as the rabbis taught:

> The gates of repentance are ever open. As the sea is always accessible, so the Holy One, blessed be He, is always accessible to the penitent.

With the sacking of the Temple by Titus in the year 70 A.D., the offering of sacrifices came to an end, and a new pattern emerged for the observance of the day: a pattern of prayer and meditation, of reading and reflection, focusing chiefly upon the forgiving mercy of God.

Though sometimes derogatively referred to as 'the black fast' the 'liturgical' colour for the day is essentially white, and though the reasons for wearing white vary from the emulation of angels to the anticipation of a shroud as being calculated to encourage repentance, the visual effect is that of a festive rather than a drab occasion.

The affliction of the soul has always been interpreted in terms of fasting, and the Day of Atonement is the one day in the Jewish religious year on which no Jew takes any kind of food or drink, save very young children, the sick or the elderly. Even so there is a very realistic and positive approach to this day on which the soul 'freed from corporeal fetters, attains the peak of its perfection in the service of God'.

The essential spirit of this approach is nowhere more vividly expressed than in a passage of Isaiah (57:15-58:14) which is read as the prophetic lesson at the morning service and thought by some to be the text of a sermon once preached on the Day of Atonement in the Temple itself.

There is nothing here of the drab or melancholy. For any who may be tempted to think that the mere fact of abstinence may win them merit in the sight of God there can be no joy. Not in the bowing of heads like bulrushes and the making of beds on sackcloth and ashes is the kind of fast the Lord requires. His concern is that the fetters of injustice should be unloosed, that food should be shared with the hungry, that the homeless should be housed and the naked clothed.

For the Christian all this has a very familiar ring. It echoes through the parable of the judgment day in Matthew (25:31-46), has been incorporated into the Lenten liturgy and paraphrased in one of the loveliest of carols, 'White Lent':

> To bow the head
> In sackcloth and in ashes
> Or rend the soul,
> Such grief is not Lent's goal;
> But to be led
> To where God's glory flashes,
> His beauty to come nigh,
> To fly, to fly,
> To fly where truth and light do lie.
>
> For is not this
> The fast that I have chosen?—
> The prophet spoke—
> To shatter every yoke

> Of wickedness
> The grievous bands to loosen,
> Oppression put to flight,
> To fight, to fight,
> To fight till every wrong's put right.

This may be good Christian teaching. It is essential Judaism. 'For transgression against God', wrote Rabbi Eleazar ben Azariah (A.D. 70-135), 'the Day of Atonement atones; but for transgressions against a fellow man the Day of Atonement does not atone so long as the sinner has not redressed the wrong done, and conciliated the man he has sinned against'.

It was another great Rabbi, Jesus of Nazareth, who also said: 'If, when you are bringing your gift to the altar, you suddenly remember that your brother has a grievance against you, leave your gift where it is before the altar. First go and make your peace with your brother, and only then come back and offer your gift' (Matthew 5:23-24).

This universal outreach of the Day of Atonement which is the quintessence of Jewish religious devotion is further emphasised by two other features of its liturgy: the first, a reading and the second, a hymn.

The reading is the book of Jonah which, since the earliest days of the liturgical tradition has been accepted as the *Haftarah* for the afternoon service of the day of Atonement. Its immediate relevance and message are obvious. If the people of a heathen city like Nineveh could repent of 'their wicked ways and habitual violence' and so win the forgiveness of God, how much more could the Jews themselves enjoy the same blessing. But that would be to see only half the message of this very remarkable book, and the less important half at that.

For the main point of the story of Jonah lies not so much in its repentance of the Ninevites as in the obduracy of the prophet. When he realised that there was no escape from the most unwelcome, most dangerous and of all improbably missions the most unlikely to succeed, Jonah finally went to Ninevah with the utmost reluctance. Then, having delivered his message, and refusing to believe either that the Ninevites would repent or that God would forgive them he sat down under a climbing gourd to watch the destruction of the city. Consumed with self-pity he could not accept that God might have pity on 'the great city of Nineveh, with its hundred and twenty thousand who cannot tell their right hand from their left, and cattle without number.' The story ends with a question mark: surely the most eloquent and searching mark of its kind in the Bible.

The hymn, the first line of which provides the title for this chapter, though of much more recent date than the book of Jonah, is nevertheless generally thought to be some eleven hundred years old. It is one of the most remarkable of all the hymns of the synagogue for its universal spirit. Like the *Yigdal* it might well find a place in any Christian hymnary.

> All the world shall come to serve thee
>   And bless thy glorious Name,
> And thy righteousness triumphant
>   The islands shall acclaim.
> And the peoples shall go seeking
>   Who knew thee not before,
> And the ends of the earth shall praise thee,
>   And tell thy greatness o'er.

They shall build for thee their altars,
　　Their idols overthrown,
And their graven gods shall shame them,
　　As they turn to thee alone,
They shall worship thee at sunrise,
　　And feel thy Kingdom's might,
And impart their understanding
　　To those astray in night.

They shall testify thy greatness
　　And of thy power speak,
And extol thee, shrined, uplifted
　　Beyond man's highest peak.
And with reverential homage,
　　Of love and wonder born,
With the ruler's crown of beauty
　　Thy head they shall adorn.

With the coming of thy Kingdom
　　The hills shall break into song,
And the islands laugh exultant
　　That they to God belong.
And all their congregations
　　So loud thy praise shall sing,
That the uttermost peoples, hearing,
　　Shall hail thee crowned King.

The day ends with a deeply moving and triumphant service known by its Hebrew name as *Neilah*. This is a shortened form of the longer phrase *Neilath She'arim* which means 'the closing of the gates' and was the name given to the prayer which used to be said when the gates of the Temple in Jerusalem were closed at the end of the day.

With the destruction of the Temple the prayer itself passed into the liturgy of the Day of Atonement and its name was given to the concluding service of the day. In this context the closing of the gates was interpreted as referring to 'the gates of heaven' which, with the books of life and death were thought figuratively to have been open since the beginning of the New

Year ten days previously. And lest this should give rise to any misunderstanding, Dr J.H. Hertz in his Commentary on the Prayer Book was careful to explain that it is 'of course, merely a poetic figure; for the gates of repentance are ever open'.

The *Neilah* Service ends with three great affirmations, proclaimed by the cantor and repeated by the congregation. The first is the *Shema:*

> Hear, O Israel, the Lord our God, the Lord is One.

This is proclaimed and repeated once only. It is followed, as we might expect, by a blessing, three times repeated:

> Blessed be His name, whose glorious Kingdom is for ever and ever.

Finally, as a kind of triumphant Amen, comes the sevenfold repetition of Elijah's cry of victory after his encounter with the prophets of Baal:

> The Lord, he is God.

Then the *Shofar*, whose wailing notes sounded the call to penitence on New Year's Day is blown again, this time with one long blast in joyous acknowledgment that the services of the day are ended, that the atonement is complete and that the festive celebration of the goodness of God can now begin.

In many synagogues today, however, this final blowing of the *Shofar* is followed by one further response from the congregation, the repetition of the hope expressed at the end of the Passover meal:

> Next year in Jerusalem.

Does this then mean that the wheel has turned full circle and that we are once more involved in the particularity of a people's history? The answer is both 'yes' and 'no'. There is a very real, and, indeed, a very proper sense in which none of us can ever escape from the particularity of our own experience. We are what we are, and until we have come to terms with that there is little point in our pretending to be anything else, and few exercises are more likely to engender awareness and acceptance of this quite fundamental truth than the proper observance of the Day of Atonement. For on that day Jews are reminded that the sins for which they most need forgiveness are those which bind them most closely to the rest of mankind, and that the God whose forgiveness they most earnestly seek is One who can have pity upon 'Nineveh, that great city with its hundred and twenty thousand who cannot tell their right hand from their left, and also much cattle'.

At the same time, it is perfectly understandable that they should turn again from the challenge of the universal to the dream of the particular and that a people who for centuries have known no country of their own save by adoption should look forward to their restoration to a land and a city whose name, Jerusalem, means 'the city of peace'.

But Jerusalem is more than a name on a map; more even than a city set on top of the Judean hills and sacred not to Jews only but to Christians and Moslems alike, a city whose potential unity seems ever to be divided by the strident claims of rival religious factions. There is another Jerusalem, a city of abiding peace, eternal in the heavens, whose builder and maker is the living God. That city is the dream in the heart of everyman, whatever his colour, creed or nationality, and whoever has glimpsed its turrets can know no lasting peace until he passes through its gates, whether this year, next year or whenever. For the gates of that city are never closed to those who know in however small a part something of the meaning of a Day of Atonement, which embraces the Ninevehs of this world no less than its Jerusalems.

'As his custom was'

I said at the beginning—and I make no apology for reverting at this stage to the first person singular—that I had no idea when I came away from my first visit to a synagogue how much a better understanding of Judaism and the history of the Jewish people might contribute to a deeper understanding of my own faith and way of life.

I was, of course, fortunate in the time at which my journey began. Already a number of books by distinguished Jewish scholars on the Jewish background to the Gospels were beginning to find their way into theological libraries. These included two volumes of *Studies in Pharisaism and the Gospels* by Israel Abrahams, a fascinating commentary on the Synoptic Gospels by Claude Montefiore and a most valuable life of Jesus of Nazareth by Joseph Klausner, to say nothing of a number of other lives of Jesus by Jewish authors which were summarised and reviewed in a valuable little book by H.D. Walker entitled *Jewish Lives of Jesus*.

There were important works too by Christian scholars, outstanding among which were George Foot Moore's classic study of Judaism in the first centuries of the Christian era; Travers Herford's illuminating essay on the Pharisees; *The Religion and Worship of the Synagogue* by Oesterley and Box; Herbert Danby's translation into English of the *Mishnah* and, representing a wide field of continental scholarship, Albert Schweitzer's *Quest for the Historical Jesus*. At the more popular level T.R. Glover's *Jesus of History* helped greatly to liberate the historical figure from the mists of christological controversy and the unreal world of nineteenth-century stained-glass windows.

At the same time the emergence of the Jewish people as a significant factor in the socio-political, cultural and economic life of the West focused attention upon the need to establish some kind of understanding of the relationship between the Jewish way of life in the New Testament and the place and treatment of the Jew in the twentieth century.

This was the period at which, in talking about the Jesus of history, we began to admit to ourselves, at times perhaps rather tentatively that 'he was of course a Jew'. The frequent addition to the qualification 'according to the flesh' may have been intended to safeguard his 'divinity'. More often than not it seemed to imply that it would be slightly improper to consider him a Jew in any other sense, and certainly not spiritually.

Today, happily, we are making progress, certainly at the junior end. Children in day and Sunday schools are increasingly encouraged to undertake 'projects' on Jews and Judaism, on the Jewish background of the New Testament, and on the historical person of Jesus himself. There are even synagogues where children and young people in the religion classes are given some basic instruction about Jesus, at least as an important figure in Jewish history. This is especially true in the State of Israel where, not least because of Christian interest in 'his land', he can hardly be ignored.

But we still have a long way to go. The statement in Saint Luke, for example (4:16), that 'he came to Nazareth where he had been brought up and went into the synagogue on the Sabbath as his custom was' is a good starting point, not least because for most of us even that begs a number of questions. The religion and worship of the synagogue are still very much a closed book to many Christians. I still vividly recall the surprise expressed by a rabbi friend of mine who, when showing a party of Christian visitors round his synagogue, overheard one member of the group say to a companion: 'why, they even use *our* psalms!'.

The Sabbath, too, remains very much an unknown quantity to those who have never conceived of it as a 'delight' nor ever experienced the 'light and rejoicing' of its observance in the Jewish home. It is difficult, too, for those who are familiar only with the Gospels, to appreciate the extent to which Jesus was a child of his time and his people, devoted to their customs and critical only of their abuse.

The truth is that since the very early days of the Church Christians have commonly failed to realise the extent to which their most treasured records bear the marks of the controversial situation out of which they emerged. This is clearly to be seen in the bitterness that has been injected into some of the recorded discussions between Jesus and those who appear only as his detractors and critics. It is a bitterness which almost certainly reflects the conflicts in which Christians so soon became involved with the 'establishment' of their day.

I would not for one moment suggest that there were no real differences between Jesus and some other teachers of his time. There was eventually sufficient to precipitate a life-and-death struggle with the religio-political authorities of his time. It is very important, however, for our understanding of Jesus himself and of the Judaism in which he was nurtured to remember that it was as a teacher, a rabbi, that he was first acclaimed and still widely recognised, especially among Jews themselves for whom acceptance of the Christian claim as to his divinity would involve an unthinkable compromise of their belief in the absolute unity of one God.

It is important also to remember that his fellow rabbis were in no sense members of a professional class. They were men who lived by their trade. Jesus was a carpenter, his friends included fishermen and even a collector of taxes. Their manner of earning their livelihood had little to do with their competence as teachers save in so far as it provided them with time for study (of the *Torah* of course) and plenty of material for parables and for gaining insight into the practical problems of daily living. This called for constant elucidation or resolution in the light of the general principles laid down in their *Torah*.

Their subject was always the same: the study of the *Torah*. Their method was essentially that of dialogue. The rabbis of Jesus' day did not write learned treatises. They engaged in seemingly interminable discussions with their teachers about the meaning of particular precepts in this or that precise situation, lightening up the process from time to time with a story, a parable or some witty aside. And since in those days they were unhampered by the 'benefits' of our modern technology and electronic gimmicks and therefore unable to depend upon the services of short-hand writers or tape-recorders they were compelled to depend upon their memories which, being much more actively exercised then than now, developed to an amazing degree many of the qualities of our contemporary computers. Thus the height of a rabbi's competence lay in the ability to quote in support of his own the opinion of some distinguished predecessor. This, of course, was 'the authority of the scribes and Pharisees'.

The Sadducees, incidentally, had no part in this kind of exercise. They recognised only the authority of the written law, the *Torah* given, as they believed, to Moses on Mount Sinai. Not for them the idea, staunchly maintained by the Pharisees that together with the written law Moses was entrusted with the beginning of an oral tradition. This, the Pharisees taught, was handed on by Moses to Joshua who passed it on (orally of course) to the Judges, from whom it passed by way of the prophets to the 'men of the Great Synagogue': the synod of 120 elders established in the time of Ezra. To these 'men of the Great Synagogue' are attributed three very important precepts: 'Be deliberate', they said, 'in judgment, raise up many disciples, and make a fence round the *Torah*'.

The making of the fence was the work of successive generations of disciples who learned to be deliberate in judgment when faced with the often perplexing and

111

always challenging task of interpreting the fundamental principles of the written law in relation to particular circumstances of their own time, in accordance with the guidelines laid down in the oral tradition.

The discussions, then, in which Jesus became involved were very largely typical of those that were going on around him all the time. Take for example the very familiar passage in Luke (10:25-37) which tells how he was approached by a 'certain lawyer' with what the New English Bible translates as a 'test question'. The translation is accurate enough. Unfortunately both its translation and the original suggest an atmosphere of hostility which was in no way essential to the point of the incident itself. For the question posed and the discussion to which it gave rise, were perfectly typical of the kind of dialogue in which the rabbis continually engaged.

There was nothing malicious about the question. Teachers then, as teachers in every age, were always interested in getting 'to the heart of the matter'. Nor was there anything ungracious in returning the question to its poser. Who has never parried a question with the reply: 'Yes, that is very interesting: but what do you think'? The fact that both were agreed as to the only possible answer is in no way surprising. Moreover the story adduced in reply to the lawyer's further question as to the identity of his neighbour, is essentially Jewish in content for it was by no means unusual for the seeming indifference of the 'establishment' to individual problems of human need to come under very much the same kind of criticism as it does today.

When not discussing particular problems the rabbis were also prone to indulge in pithy sayings and ethical

112

precepts of which the Sermon on the Mount is an outstanding collection. Whether that 'Sermon' was spoken at one time or compiled by the evangelist from sayings delivered on many occasions we may never know for certain. Matthew treats it in one way, and Luke another. Whatever the answer, the content is essentially Jewish.

Consider, for example, the teaching of Jesus on prayer which in Matthew finds its place in the Sermon but in Luke (11:2-4) is given in response to a request from his disciples. His warning against the perils of ostentation, his emphasis upon privacy and the need to avoid 'heathen babblings' is entirely in the spirit of the best Jewish teaching about prayer both before and since his time. As for the actual prayer he taught them, now universally known as the Lord's Prayer, it is entirely in the spirit and idiom of prayers which were already in general use in his day and from which Dr Israel Abrahams compiled the following:

> Our Father, who art in heaven, Hallowed be Thine exalted Name in the world which Thou didst create according to Thy will. May Thy Kingdom and Thy lordship come speedily, and be acknowledged by all the world, that Thy Name may be praised in all eternity. May Thy will be done in Heaven, and also on earth give tranquility of spirit to those that fear Thee, yet in all things do what seemeth good to Thee. Let us enjoy the bread daily apportioned to us. Forgive us, our Father, for we have sinned. Forgive also all who have done us injury; even as we also forgive all. And lead us not into temptation, but keep us far from all evil. For thine is the greatness and the power and the dominion, the victory and the majesty, yea, all in Heaven and on earth. Thine is the Kingdom and Thou are lord of all being for ever, Amen.

Where, then, is all this leading? Not, let me hasten to explain, to yet another life of Jesus. Nor is it merely to suggest that he was just one more among a host of teachers of similar outlook and comparable insight. That, at least, he certainly was. It should in no way detract from our appreciation of either his teaching or his person to see them in their natural rabbinic setting.

The true greatness of Jesus, after all, lies not in the originality of what he taught but in the extent to which that teaching found its embodiment in his life. For him, as we have just seen, the essence of Judaism, as indeed of eternal life, lay in the love of God and of one's neighbour, and that love, as everything about him clearly showed, could not be enclosed by any fence of interpretative ingenuity.

It was this that brought him in the end to the cross. Men can and do argue about principles. What else are politics about? So long as the issue is confined to what seems at the time and in any given circumstances to be both practical and possible, it is normally acceptable. It is when we pass from the relative to the absolute that difficulties arise. Few things are more terrifying than the absolute demand of that total loving which lies at the heart of the *Torah*.

It was the growing resistance of some sections of the community not merely to certain aspects of his teaching but to the disturbing impact upon themselves of the inexplicable nature of his person which led to his being arraigned before the leaders of both the religious and political establishments of his day. His rejection, condemnation and death followed inevitably. In the end even his closest friends could endure it no more and found themselves driven, in spite of themselves, to deny that they ever knew him and to leave him to the solitary death from which, as they came eventually to believe, he rose again on the third day.

114

But that is another story. My concern here is with the subsequent failure of a predominantly Gentile Christian Church to recognise two things: the first is that Jesus was not an enemy, but a loyal and devoted son of the synagogue to which he went, not only on a certain Sabbath in Nazareth, but always, 'as his custom was', and secondly that his death was not the crime of a whole people, but the outcome of a set of circumstances, political and religious, which have had their counterpart, I suppose, in every generation before and since, and not among Jews only.

No one, I think, has ever made this second point more forcefully than Dorothy Sayers in the Introduction to her play-cycle: *The Man born to be King*. There, talking of the problems of translating the record of events of two thousand years ago into a contemporary idiom, she wrote:

Technically, the swiftest way to produce the desirable sense of shock, is the use in drama of modern speech and a determined historical realism about the characters. Herod the Great was no monstrous enemy of God: he was a soldier of fortune and a political genius—a savage but capable autocrat, whose jealousy and ungovernable temper had involved him in a prolonged domestic wretchedness. Matthew the Publican was a contemptible little quisling official, fleecing his own countrymen in the service of the occupying power and enriching himself in the process, until something came to change his heart (though not, presumably his social status or his pronunciation). Pontius Pilate was a provincial governor, with a very proper desire to carry out Imperial justice, but terrified (as better men than he have been before and since) of questions in the House, commissions of inquiry and what may be generically called 'Whitehall'. Caiaphas was the ecclesiastical politician, appointed (like one of Hitler's bishops) by a heathen government, expressly that he might collaborate with the New Order and see that the Church toed the line drawn by the State; we have seen something of Caiaphas lately. As for the Elders of the Synagogue, they are to be found on every Parish Council—always highly respectable, often quarrelsome, and sometimes in a crucifying mood.

Dorothy Sayers was writing in 1943. Already a new translation was being written in the unfolding tragedy of the Nazi persecution of Jews which in its turn was but the intensification of what had already befallen the Jews of eastern Europe under the Czarist regime a generation earlier. The horror and the hope inherent in both for the Christian must surely be the dawning awareness of the fact that the Christ for whose first crucifixion 'the Jews' were mistakenly held responsible by his followers, has been crucified again and again in the sufferings inflicted by those who proudly professed his name upon those whose customs he was careful to observe.

No one has seen this more clearly or presented it more movingly than the greatest of contemporary Jewish artists, Marc Chagall, who in the years between 1938 and 1951 painted a series of 'Crucifixions' in each of which the figure on the cross was identified as a Jew by the prayer shawl draped round his loins, and in one of them by the phylacteries bound in the traditional way round his forehead and his left forearm. And if that were not enough the background to the cross is filled with glimpses of the *stetl*, the typical Russian-Jewish village in which Chagall himself was born.

In one in particular, the *White Crucifixion*, painted in 1938, the year in which all the synagogues in Germany were destroyed by fire in one night, Chagall depicts the sacking of the *stetl*. Flames can be seen engulfing the synagogue. There is a Scroll of the Law also being consumed by flames. In another corner a man is escaping with a Scroll in his arms and in the centre a boatload of refugees is fleeing across the river.

In 1938 Chagall was not to know what we were all so soon to see in the spread of the flames which destroyed the *stetl* to the crematoria of the Nazi extermination camps through which between five and six million Jews, men, women and children, went to their deaths. In their midst, I cannot but believe, was one 'like unto the Son of Man', the servant of whom the prophet sang and of whom, together with his fellow Jews thus crucified before our eyes, it is surely no exaggeration to say that 'the chastisement of our peace was upon them' and to pray that 'by their stripes' we too may be healed.

And if that seems perhaps a little abstract and remote the following prayer, found when the largest of the Nazi concentration camps for women, Ravensbruck, was liberated, might make it more immediate and relevant. Written on a piece of wrapping paper, it carried no clue as to its source. It could equally well have been the prayer of a Jewess or a Christian:

> O Lord, remember not only the men and women of goodwill but also those of illwill. But do not remember all the suffering they have inflicted upon us; remember the fruits we bought, thanks to this suffering, our comradeship, our loyalty, our humility, the courage, the generosity, the greatness of heart which has grown out of this; and when they come to judgment, let all the fruits that we have borne be their forgiveness.

Guidelines for the Future

It is a far cry from the synagogues of Galilee to which Jesus used to go 'as his custom was', and from the lakeside slopes where, as tradition has it, he delivered his Sermon on the Mount, to the hell of Ravensbruck which inspired an unknown concentration-camp victim to pray for the forgiveness of her enemies and the burning of the *stetl* which provided Chagall with the background for his 'crucifixions'. But the links are there for all to see. And in the forging of these links Christians, however unwittingly, have played a major part.

I said at the outset that my early studies in the origins and development of antisemitism had filled me, as a Christian, with a deep sense of shame and humiliation. In this I was far from alone. The shock of the Nazi persecution of the Jews produced widespread protest at such blatant crimes against humanity. But protest was not enough. The great need was, and remains, to safeguard mankind against the repetition of atrocities which bring disaster upon the persecutors no less than upon the persecuted.

First, however, it was necessary to unravel the cause. In the months immediately preceding the outbreak of war in September 1939 I remember meeting with a group of biologists and sociologists who were chiefly concerned to expose the fallacies of the myth of *racial* superiority and inferiority upon which the whole Nazi ideology was based. Much time was spent in discussing the relevance or irrelevance of measurement of skulls, arms and other physical features. It was all very interesting and in its way valuable, not least in preparing the way for the eventual publication by UNESCO of a series of pamphlets which, on authoritative scientific grounds, effectively disposed of what one writer on racialism has described as 'man's most dangerous myth'.

One incidental result of these studies was to focus the spotlight of meaninglessness on the word 'antisemitism' itself which nowhere appears earlier than 1879. This is hardly surprising since there is really no such thing as 'semitism' to oppose. Strictly speaking the word 'semitic' applies only to a family of languages which embraces both Hebrew and Arabic. In current parlance, however, 'antisemitism' has little to do with linguistic likes and dislikes. It has one connotation only. To be antisemitic means quite simply to be anti-Jewish, and the roots of that antipathy go very deep.

As deep, in fact, as the beginnings of Christianity itself. Jews, as I pointed out at the beginning, have always been something of a problem to their neighbours. The dissenter, or the non-conformist, always is. But with the emergence of the Church from the synagogue, with the virtual separation of Christianity from its

Judaic roots, the problem assumed an altogether new dimension.

'The origin of antisemitism' wrote Dr James Parkes in his earliest book on the subject: *The Jew and his neighbour* (first published in 1930), 'lies, unconsciously and unintentionally, in the interpretation of the Old Testament current in the early Church, and in the picture of the Jews, as a rebellious people who had crucified the Messiah and still refused to believe in Him, which was continually repeated from the Christian pulpit'.

In explaining his use of the words 'unconsciously and unintentionally', Dr Parkes pointed out that 'the same centuries which saw the theologians draw the most awful picture of Jewish perfidy and baseness saw the friendliest relations between Jews and their neighbours, and the Jews as a perfectly normal section of society'. This was hardly surprising, for during the early centuries of the current era Christians and Jews had this at least in common that both were members of minority religious groups which, unlike the majority of the conformists of their day, refused to participate in the simplest form of emperor worship imposed upon all subject peoples. Together they lived under the same threat of persecution and death.

It was during this period, however, that the outlines of the now universally accepted caricature of 'the Jews' were clearly drawn and the foundations of those discriminatory policies which eventually resulted in the reduction of Jews to the status of second-class citizens firmly laid. This process was accelerated with the accession of the Emperor Constantine in the year 313 A.D. At the outset of his reign he declared the Empire to be Christian and almost at once began to introduce anti-Jewish provisions into his new legislation.

The study of the religious roots of antisemitism was taken further by Dr Parkes himself in two still outstandingly important volumes: *The Conflict between the Church and the Synagogue* (1934) and *The Jew in the Medieval Community* (1938). He was followed by a very distinguished French Jewish scholar and historian, Jules Isaac, who on being dismissed by the Nazis from the senior post in the French schools system, escaped to Provence in unoccupied France. There, being already too old for military service and too great a man merely to indulge in recriminations, he devoted the later years of his life to exposing the antipathy to Judaism and things Jewish on the part of the writers of the Gospels in particular. Begun in 1943, as he himself wrote, 'in the midst of a life, already threatened, hunted and soon to be ravaged and run to earth', his study was completed in 1946 and published in 1948 under the title *Jésus et Israel*. Its impact, though neither as immediate nor as far-reaching as its author hoped (what author ever is satisfied with the impact of his works?), nevertheless has had a marked influence upon the subsequent development of concern on the part of Christians, catholic and protestant alike, at the extent of Christian responsibility for the origin and development of those anti-Jewish attitudes which led directly to the fires of the *stetl*, to the hell of the Nazi holocaust, and the crucifixion of his people by the professed followers of the crucified.

The story of what has happened in this particular respect since the collapse of the 'Reich which was to last a thousand years' is too long to be told here in detail.

Nevertheless it is so much a part of the *raison d'être* of this book that some of the landmarks must be indicated, if only to encourage the reader to explore the territory in greater detail for himself.

During the closing stages of the 1939-45 war plans began to be formulated for the holding of a first-ever International Conference of Christians and Jews at as early a date as possible. This eventually took place in Oxford in August 1946. Its theme was not, as might have been expected, the problem of antisemitism, but 'Freedom, Justice and Responsibility'. It was a brave gesture: an acknowledgment that what the world most needed, in the aftermath of so great a cataclysm, was co-operation on the part of Christians and Jews in particular in the advancement of those fundamental moral and ethical principles which lie at the heart of the Judaeo-Christian tradition.

'Oxford 1946', however, was only a beginning. If the co-operation implicit in its recommendations was to be effectively achieved it was essential that the traditional causes of misunderstanding between Christians and Jews be broached without delay. A further Conference was therefore planned for the following year. Its theme was to be antisemitism, and its venue Seeligsberg, high above the Ruetli where the first Swiss cantonal federation was established in 1291.

To Seeligsberg came Jules Isaac, and there, not surprisingly, he played a major role in the formulation of what very soon came to be known as the Ten Points of Seeligsberg. These ten points, together with a brief address to the Churches, remain to this day a succinct and useful guide for Christian teachers who are aware of a problem and anxious to ensure that their presentation of the Jewish background of Christianity shall be free from the distortions and inaccuracies of earlier generations.

This document found its way back to the Vatican where it was accorded a *'nihil obstat'* and to the World Council of Churches where it played some part in helping to direct the attention of successive Assemblies of the World Council to the importance for the Church as well as for the Jewish community of fostering sound relationships of mutual understanding and goodwill.

So far as the World Council of Churches is concerned the process began at its first Assembly in Amsterdam in 1948. It continued through a series of consultations, through the publication in 1954 of a symposium entitled: *The Church and the Jewish People* and through successive General Assemblies at Evanston, U.S.A. (1954), New Delhi, India (1961) and at Uppsala in Sweden in 1968.

The Uppsala Assembly recalled the New Delhi request to 'examine educational and devotional materials with a view to eliminating any misrepresentation of Judaism and the Jewish people'. It reported 'with satisfaction that the Assembly resolution had been implemented by a number of Churches', and encouraged those which had not yet acted to do so.

The Council's Committee on the Church and the Jewish People recommended co-operation with national councils of Christians and Jews; encouraged programmes of education about Jewish culture and teaching and about synagogue worship and religious practice. Co-operation with Jewish scholars was suggested in order to relate the Scriptures to Judaism as a living faith. The Committee also testified to the abiding reality of the Jewish people as an element within the purpose of God. Finally it recommended that the Church should seek 'by all possible means to reach deeper levels of understanding of the Jews, of Judaism, of the meaning of the State of Israel, and of God's purposes concerning them as revealed in the Scriptures'.

On the Catholic side the story began with certain changes in the Good Friday Litany. There the faithful were bidden to pray for the *'perfidis Judaei'*. Whatever its original connotation *'perfidis'* had come to be interpreted as 'perfidious'. Understandably the phrase 'perfidious Jews' had long been a source of grave offence to the Jewish community. An initial step was taken to put this right when a directive was issued explaining that the word was to be understood as meaning 'faithless' in the sense of being 'without the faith'. Later in 1958 the phrase was dropped altogether at the bidding of Pope John XXIII.

Of much greater significance, however, was the outcome of a meeting in 1960 between Jules Isaac and Pope John XXIII. Madame Claire Huchet-Bishop, a close friend and colleague of Jules Isaac, in a biographical introduction to her translation of his last book: *The Teaching of Contempt*, tells how 'the two venerable men sat side by side in a lengthy, earnest and friendly conversation. Professor Isaac made a brief summary of the results of his research, and presented his request. He pointed out that although there had been a reversal of attitude on the part of many individual Catholics, both during and after the war, nothing conclusive had yet been done. There was a crying need for the voice of the head of the Church to be heard, solemnly and forever condemning "the teaching of contempt". Then Professor Isaac presented his own practical suggestion, the creation of a subcommission in the Vatican Council, especially empowered to study this question. The Pope, who had been listening attentatively, and sympathetically, declared spontaneously, "I have been thinking about that ever since you began to speak".'

There can be little doubt that this meeting helped to ensure the inclusion in the documents promulgated by the Vatican Council of a declaration on the Church and the Jewish People. Though its passage through the Council was by no means easy, it opened the way for a complete new approach by the Catholic Church to the whole question of the relations, historic and contemporary, with the Jewish people.

While not without its limitations, the document was welcomed both in its intentions and general content by Jews and Christians alike. Particularly welcome was its affirmation that 'what happened to Christ in his passion was not to be charged against all Jews, without distinction, then alive, nor against the Jews of today. Jews should not be presented as rejected by God or accursed, as if this flowed from the Holy Scripture' and that 'all should see to it that in catechetical works and preaching nothing was taught that was not conformable to the truth of the Gospel and the spirit of Christ'. Condemnation of 'hatred, persecution and displays of antisemitism directed against Jews at any time or by any one', was balanced by the commendation of 'mutual understanding and respect arising from biblical and theological studies and fraternal dialogue'.

Declarations of principle by ecclesiastical assemblies are one thing, however. Their implementation at rank-and-file level is quite another matter.

The Declaration, therefore, was followed in December 1974 by the issue of a set of 'Guidelines and suggestions for implementing the Conciliar declaration'. Prepared by the Vatican Commission for Relations with Jews these Guidelines start with a reminder that 'although Christianity springs from Judaism, taking from it certain essential elements of its faith and divine cult, the gap between them was deepened more and more, to such an extent that Christian and Jew hardly knew each other'.

'Christians must therefore strive', the document continues, 'to acquire a better knowledge of the basic components of the religious tradition of Judaism, they must strive to learn by what essential traits the Jews define themselves in the light of their own religious experience'.

Though primarily concerned with 'launching or developing sound relations between Catholics and their Jewish brethren' the practical proposals set out in the Guidelines are of general application. They relate to 'different essential areas of the Church's life'.

The first of these is the need to establish 'real dialogue' which 'presupposes that each side wishes to increase and deepen its knowledge of the other', and 'demands respect for the other as he is; above all, respect for his faith and his religious convictions'.

Two points in the development of these basic theses have given rise to some uneasiness in Jewish circles. The first is the statement that 'in view of her divine mission, and her very nature, the Church must preach Jesus Christ to the world'. The second is the suggestion that 'in whatever circumstances as shall prove possible and mutually acceptable, one might encourage a common meeting in the presence of God, in prayer and silent meditation'.

Those who know anything of Jewish history will know how Jews in every generation have resisted joint worship with people of other faiths. This explains the rather cool reception accorded to the idea of 'a common meeting ... in prayer and silent meditation'. Similarly the reference to preaching Jesus Christ has been taken to imply the kind of proselytism or missionary activity from which Jews have so often suffered so much.

It is essential, however, in a document of this kind that the most careful attention be given to questions of context: the context of the document as a whole as well as the context of everyone of its parts.

While it would be unreasonable to expect the Church, whether Catholic or Protestant, to deny so vital a part of its *raison d'être* as the preaching of the Gospel, it is essential to recognise that this statement of the Christian's duty is immediately followed by the important reminder that 'lest the witness of Catholics to Jesus Christ should give offence to Jews, they must take care to live and spread their Christian faith while maintaining the strictest respect for religious liberty in line with the teaching of the Second Vatican Council'.

Equally the commendation of 'common meetings in prayer and silent meditation' is amply safeguarded by the emphasis upon 'possible and mutually acceptable' circumstances.

The second major area of the Church's life in which the Guidelines found room for developing mutual understanding is the liturgy. Here the document recalls 'the existing links between the Christian liturgy and the Jewish liturgy'. Some of those links I have already tried to point out. The others, and they are many, are for the finding.

Here we are reminded of the need 'to acquire a better understanding of whatever in the Old Testament retains its own perpetual value', of the need to emphasise 'the continuity of our faith with that of the earlier Covenant' and of the need to ensure that 'homilies based upon liturgical [readings from the Scriptures] will not distort their meaning especially when it is a question of passages which seem to show the Jewish people as such in an unfavourable light'. The need for care in translation is also emphasised especially in relation to 'those phrases and passages which Christians, if not well informed, might misunderstand because of prejudice'.

An important footnote on this section draws attention to particular examples. 'Thus', it reads, 'the formula "the Jews" in Saint John, sometimes, according to the context means "the leaders of the Jews" or "the adversaries of Jesus", terms which express better the thought of the evangelist and avoid appearing to arraign the Jewish people as such. Another example is the use of the words "pharisee" and "pharisaism" which have taken on a largely pejorative meaning'.

Teaching and education, both at elementary and advanced levels, constitute a third important area of development. Research in the fields of exegesis, theology, history and sociology; the creation of chairs of Jewish studies and the encouragement of collaboration with Jewish scholars all hold out good and exciting prospects.

Finally, there is a reminder that common to the Jewish and Christian tradition, and 'founded on the word of God' is a shared awareness of the value of the human person, created in the image of God. 'Love of the same God' the document continues 'must show itself in effective action for the good of mankind. In the spirit of the prophets, Jews and Christians will work willingly together, seeking social justice and peace at every level—local, national and international'.

It is a high ideal: a dream as inspiring as that of Martin Luther King. It brings us back full circle to the first International Conference of Christians and Jews in Oxford in 1946 with its theme of 'Freedom, Justice and Responsibility'.

That was thirty years ago. The euphoria of the immediate post-war situation has today given place almost everywhere to cynicism and frustration. Freedom is confused with license, justice pursued by unjust means, and responsibility irresponsibly exercised. But hope dies hard. Else why have I bothered to write this essay?

As one who had quite a bit to do with the planning and organisation of that Conference and who has spent the past thirty years in an almost infinitely varied 'follow-up' exercise I have time and again been immensely stimulated by one of its, for me, most vivid memories.

It is of a service held in the Chapel of the College where the Conference took place. They attended who would. Much of the detail has gone with the wind, but one thing I think I shall never forget. After days of almost incessant activity (I was one of the Conference Secretaries) the opening words of the sermon set the whole venture in an entirely new and immensely refreshing dimension. They were a quotation from Henry Vaughan, the seventeenth-century English mystic:

> I saw Eternity the other night
> Like a great ring of pure and endless light,
> All calm, as it was bright,
> And round beneath it, Time in hours, days, years,
> Driv'n by the spheres
> Like a vast shadow moved; in which the world
> And all her train were hurled.

It is true, as the Vatican guidelines laconically remind us in the brief concluding section that 'there is still a long road ahead'.

It is also true, as I have been reminded over the years by Rabbi Tarfon who lived in the second century that: 'The day is short, and the work is great, and the labourers are sluggish, and the reward is much and the Master is urgent'. He used also to say: 'It is not thy duty to complete the work, but neither art thou free to desist from it'.

But it is also true that the pressure of

> Time in hours, days, years,
> Driv'n by the spheres
> Like a vast shadow

is not the ultimate pressure. For Jews and Christians live, not in one world but in two, one temporal and the other eternal. And the 'miracle of miracles' is that for both Christians and Jews those two worlds are not separated by some arbitrary sequence in time. The temporal is for ever being caught up into and transformed by the eternal, and the gates between them are never closed.

In that faith we live. By the hope it inspires we progress. In the love which embraces both we find our renewal and our fulfilment.

Postscript

All this, of course, has some very practical implications: there are books to be read, contacts to be made, visits to be arranged.

Happily there are people in many countries whose pleasure it is to help with any or all of these. Quoted below are the addresses of twelve organisations for promoting understanding and friendship between Christians and Jews.

But if an organisation sounds rather remote or formidable: why not consult your local priest or your minister; ask your librarian for suggestions for further reading (I have appended a few basic suggestions of my own) and if you happen to live in an area where there is a Jewish community, do not hesitate to get in touch with the local minister or Rabbi.

And if, for any reason, all else fails and you think I might be able to help, by all means write to me and I will do my best. Address your letter to the Council of Christians and Jews in London at: 41 Cadogan Gardens, London SW3 2TD.

Further Reading

Had he been alive today the author of the Book of Ecclesiastes might well have written: 'Of the making of bibliographies there is no end, and much study of them leads to constant frustration'. So many books are written, so many are published at ever increasing prices, and so many are out of print almost before the would-be reader knows of their existence or sets out in pursuit of them.

This note, then, makes no claim to completeness, nor does it hold out any sort of guarantee that any of the books it mentions is still available other than through a good library service. All I can say is that he who is fortunate enough to run to earth any or all of them, whether through a book shop (new or second-hand) or through any library, will find them well-worth reading.

The Bible

Everyone will have his or her own Bible, of whatever translation, old or new. Most readers, I suspect, will be familiar with this or that commentary. Here then I mention only three items likely to be of special interest to the non-Jewish reader:

(i) *The Holy Scriptures*:
The standard Jewish translation of the Hebrew Bible into English, published by the Jewish Publications Society of America (Philadelphia) and the Cambridge University Press (in England). The books in this version are arranged in accordance with the three-fold division of the Hebrew scriptures into the Law, the Prophets and the Writings. It also contains the details of the Synagogue lectionary for Sabbaths and Festivals.

(ii) *The Pentateuch*:
The first five books of the Hebrew Bible in Hebrew with the English translation (as above) and a commentary by the former Chief Rabbi: the Rev'd Dr J.H. Hertz: an invaluable door and window opener into the understanding of the Jewish approach to and understanding of the Scriptures. Still in print and published by the Soncino Press.

(iii) *Commentaries*:
These are legion, but there is a series of *Commentaries on the Books of the Bible* with Hebrew text, English translation and commentary which any interested reader will find of great value. The series (one volume per book) is published by the Soncino Press, Hindhead, Surrey.

Prayer Books

Here again the selection is large and varied. Basic, however, is the *Authorised Daily Prayer Book* of the United Hebrew Congregations of the British Commonwealth. In Hebrew (with English translation by the late Rev'd S. Singer) it may be likened to the Anglican Book of Common Prayer or the Daily Missal of the Catholic Church. Published by Eyre & Spotiswoode.

An invaluable aid to the study of the Prayer Books is a revised edition with commentary by the late Rabbi Dr J.H. Hertz, published by Shapiro Vallentine & Co. London.

Other important works in this field are the volumes of Festival Prayers, published by Routledge & Kegan Paul Ltd. and two volumes recently published by the Union of Liberal and Progressive Synagogues, London. The first of these, *The Service of the Heart*, contains a series of services for Sabbaths and daily use, while the second, *Gates of Repentance*, covers the services for New Year and Day of Atonement.

Perhaps the most popular and most readily available in a wide range of editions with and without commentary is the Haggadah, the order of service for Passover. For general purposes the Cecil Roth edition published by the Soncino Press is perhaps the most helpful for the non-Jewish reader, but those who look for something more glamorous from the point of view both of text and illustrations will surely find it in *A Feast of History* by Chaim Raphael, published by Weidenfeld & Nicholson.

General Books

1. On *Judaism* in general the following will be found of great value:

> *Judaism: A Historical Presentation*—Isidore Epstein, Penguin Books
> *Judaism: A Portrait*—Leon Roth, Faber & Faber
> *This is my God*—Herman Wouk, Jonathan Cape
> *Judaism* (Two volumes for the more advanced reader)—George Foot Moore, Harvard University Press
> *Principles of the Jewish Faith*—Louis Jacobs, Vallentine Mitchell

2. On the *Synagogue and Jewish Worship*:

> *The Synagogue—its History and Function*—Isaac Levy, Vallentine Mitchell
>
> *The Religion and Worship of the Synagogue*—Oesterley & Box, Pitman (long since out of print but worth pursuing through a library)
>
> *The Jewish Festivals*—S.M. Lehrman, Shapiro Vallentine
>
> *Guides to the Festivals: The Sabbath* (S. Goldman); *Rosh Hashana* (Louis Jacobs); *Succoth* (I.M. Fabricant); *Chanukah and Purim* (I.M. Fabricant); *Chanukah and Purim* (S.M. Lehrman); *Passover* (Isaac Levy); *Shavuoth* (Chaim Pearl); *Minor Festivals and Fasts* (Chaim Pearl)—published separately by Jewish Chronicle Publications, or together in presentation case.

3. *Judaism and Christianity*

> *The Foundation of Judaism and Christianity*—James Parkes, Vallentine Mitchell
>
> *Prelude to Dialogue*—James Parkes, Vallentine Mitchell
>
> *The Teaching of Contempt*—Jules Isaac, Holt-Rinehart-Winston, New York
>
> *Faith and Fratricide*—Rosemary Ruether, Search Press (London)
>
> *Sweeter than Honey*—Peter Schneider, SCM Press

... and, one might add, a host of others. Any of the books noted here will serve at least as 'starters' while most of them may well prove to be meals in their own right. I can only conclude by saying not merely 'good hunting' but 'good reading' also!

International Council of Christians and Jews: list of member organisations:

Austria: Aktion gegen den Antisemitismus in Oesterreich
Vienna 1180, Backenbruennlgasse 5/4

Belgium: National Secretary of the Jewish Christian Relations Section of the Commission for Ecumenical Problems of the Roman Catholic Bishops
3000 Leuven, Dekenstraat 32

Brazil: Conselho de Fraternidade Cristao-Judaica
Rua Martim Francisco, 738 casa 01, V. Barque
01226 Sao Paulo

Canada: Canadian Council of Christians and Jews
Room 506, 229 Yonge Street
Toronto, Ontario

France: Amitie Judeo-Chretienne de France
11 rue d'Enghien, 75010 Paris

Germany: Deutscher Koordinierungsrat der Gesellschaften fuer Christlich-Juedische Zusammenarbeit
6 Frankfurt a.M., Mittelweg 10

Holland: Het Leerhuis
Hendrik van Vlandenstraat 17, Vreeland (U)

Israel: Israel Interfaith Committee
P.O. Box 2028, 12a Khoresh Street
Jerusalem

Italy: Amicizia Ebraico-Christiana di Firenze
Via delle Terme 21, 50123 Florence

Switzerland: Christlich-Juedische Arbeitsgemeinschaft in der Schweiz
Hirzenstrasse 10, 4125 Riehen/Basel

United Kingdom: Council of Christians and Jews
41 Cadogan Gardens, London SW3 2TD

U.S.A.: National Conference of Christians and Jews
43 West 57th Street
New York, NY 10019

Acknowledgments

Grateful acknowledgment is made to Thames & Hudson for the quotation from *The Tree of Life* by Roger Cook; to Canon F.W. Dillistone for the quotation from the 1968 Brampton Lectures: *Traditional Symbols in the Contemporary World*; to Shapiro Vallentine for the quotations from *Commentary on the Daily Prayer Book* by Dr J.H. Hertz; to Edward Goldstone for the quotation from *Jewish Life in the Middle Ages* by Dr Israel Abrahams; to Faber & Faber for the quotation from *Judaism: A Portrait* by Leon Roth; to Cambridge University Press for the quotation from *Studies in Pharisaism and the Gospels* by Dr Israel Abrahams; to Gollancz for the quotation from *The Man born to be King* by Dorothy Sayers; to SCM Press for the quotation from *The Jew and his Neighbour* by Dr James Parkes; and to Holt, Reinhardt for the quotation from *The Teaching of Contempt* by Dr James Parkes.

Printed in the Republic of Ireland